Los Angeles Daily News

OUT OF THIS WORLD

HOW THE **LOS ANGELES DODGERS** CAPTURED BACK-TO-BACK WORLD SERIES CHAMPIONSHIPS

SPECIAL COMMEMORATIVE EDITION

This book is available in quantity at special discounts for your group or organization.
For further information, contact:

Triumph Books LLC
814 North Franklin Street
Chicago, Illinois 60610
Phone: (312) 337-0747
www.triumphbooks.com

Printed in U.S.A.
ISBN: 978-1-63727-047-9

Content packaged by Mojo Media, Inc.
Joe Funk: Editor
Jason Hinman: Creative Director

Southern California News Group
Ron Hasse, President & Publisher
Frank Pine, Executive Editor
Tom Moore, Executive Sports Editor
Caroline Wong, Sr. Director of Marketing
Julie Corlette, Marketing Manager
Michele Cardon and Dean Musgrove, Photo Editors

Front and Back Cover Photos by AP Images

CONTENTS

Introduction

By Jim Alexander | November 1, 2025

Dave Roberts said it after the Dodgers had swept Milwaukee in the National League Championship Series:

"Before this season they were saying the Dodgers are ruining baseball. Let's get four more wins and really ruin baseball."

Saturday night, this ruining baseball business was tough, time-consuming and tense. But evidently, the National Pastime will never be the same.

Kidding.

But if you want to refer to these Dodgers as a dynasty, as the first repeat World Series champions in 25 years, winners of three in six years and participants in five World Series over the last decade ... who on earth can argue at this point?

And for all of their offensive woes over the last week, especially with men in scoring position, the way they stole this one was classic in itself.

The Toronto Blue Jays were five outs away from their first championship in 32 years. The fans' pent up emotions were spilling over, with a 4-2 lead and the giddy anticipation of a parade of their very own.

And then Max Muncy hit a solo home run in the eighth, and the unlikeliest of souls, Miguel Rojas, hit his first of the postseason with one out in the ninth, and the champagne in the Toronto clubhouse remained on ice.

And Will Smith, postseason hero, put this game, and this season, on ice with his second home run of the postseason with two outs in the 11th inning, a shot down the left field line that officially traveled 366 feet but undoubtedly reverberated three time zones away, and probably was felt throughout baseball.

The Dodgers won this with Yoshinobu Yamamoto playing the part of Walker Buehler, a starter coming to the rescue with 2⅔ innings of scoreless relief. They won it despite going 1 for 11 with runners in scoring position on Saturday night, extending their output in such situations to 9 for 47 for the series, a .191 average. (That included a bases-loaded, one-out situation in the top of the 10th in which they were scoreless.

And yet they won a World Series. We can't say it was improbable, but there were times during this series when it seemed that way. The Blue Jays were that good, and that tough and gritty and efficient.

The narrative all along, and the reference to which Roberts was referring, was the notion that the Dodgers' payroll, $350,024,106 and first in the majors according to Spotrac, gave them a humongous edge over everybody else. (The New York Mets, of course, had almost as high a payroll and missed the postseason altogether. And, for what it's worth, the Blue Jays' payroll of $255,230,405 American, according to Spotrac, was No. 7 in the big leagues – and converts to $358,317,658 in Canadian dollars, which is what their players spend when they're at home.)

Remember, too, that the Blue Jays are owned by Canadian heavyweight Rogers Communications. They were among those taking out ads imploring the Blue Jays to "bring it home."

Instead, the Commissioner's Trophy will be coming back to Southern California, and instead of a parade down Yonge Street, Toronto's major thoroughfare, the double-decker buses will again be rumbling down Broadway in the next few days.

And if you want to crack that the supposed best team money could buy couldn't buy a hit with runners in scoring position when they needed it most ... well, in this case solo home runs count as clutch hitting, too.

And maybe we need to get beyond the payroll narrative.

Manager Dave Roberts was asked about it in his briefing before Saturday's game. The Dodgers aren't the only ones who spend large sums on payroll, obviously. But there are – there have to be – other ways to create an advantage.

Los Angeles Dodgers players swarm pitcher Yoshinobu Yamamoto on the mound after recording the final out in Game 7 against the Toronto Blue Jays. (AP Images)

"I think that people just overlook the fact that every year we probably have the top-five farm system in baseball," he said. "This year I think we probably have the No. 1 or No. 2. We pick at the bottom of the draft every year, towards the bottom, and we still have young guys, whether by way of trade or development, that continue to help contribute."

Player development, in other words, matters a lot. Skill at putting together a roster does, as well – and for all of the grief This Space has given President of Baseball Operations Andrew Friedman and General Manager Brandon Gomes for the moves they didn't make to add relief pitching help at the July 31 trade deadline, obviously it worked out.

"So on the business side," Roberts continued, "I think that we do a great job of marketing our organization. So it's pretty buttoned up. I think we have great people and obviously great ownership too."

The Dodgers were a streaky team all season, romping to a big division lead through June, and spending the next three months spinning their wheels, largely because of that sometimes dysfunctional bullpen. They had some streakiness offensively, too.

And after storming through the first three rounds of the postseason – going 9-1 against the Cincinnati Reds, Philadelphia Phillies and the Brewers – they struggled against a Toronto team that was fundamentally sound with a consistent offensive approach.

But there was some grit in these guys, too. They regrouped after losing Games 4 and 5 at home, and became the ninth team to win Games 6 and 7 on the road and with them the championship.

So they've made history, they've earned the right to be a dynasty ... and if you want to start talking three-peat, go ahead. I suspect Pat Riley, credited with trademarking that term, won't mind. ■

WORLD SERIES GAME 1
October 24, 2025 | Toronto, Ontario
BLUE JAYS 11, DODGERS 4

Rude Awakening

Blue Jays Erupt Against Dodgers' Bullpen, Win World Series Opener

By Jim Alexander

Toronto Blue Jays manager John Schneider made the observation Friday afternoon, before his first World Series game as a manager, that he and his coaches weren't treating this as a best-of-seven.

"To me and the coaches kind of every game is a – there's seven one-game series, basically, is how we're looking at it," he said. "So every night is going to be a different way to go about it. I think that we have the roster and personnel flexibility to do that differently every night."

And maybe that's how Dodgers manager Dave Roberts and his coaches should be looking at it now. After dominating the first three rounds of baseball's postseason, the Dodgers are now faced with a moving target.

Things got ugly quickly Friday night, with an abomination of a sixth inning – highlighted (or, depending on how you look at it, marred) by the first pinch-hit grand slam in World Series history by Addison Barger – allowing Toronto to get the jump on the defending champs, 11-4.

This could suggest two things. First, this is not going to be the walkover many observers (but, ahem, not this one) said it would be. Second, more performances like that and the defending champs aren't going to be champs much longer.

The latter is likely an overreaction. One game getting out of hand doesn't necessarily suggest a trend.

As for the first part? Don't be so surprised. Toronto won 94 games in the regular season, finishing ahead of the New York Yankees on a tiebreaker and then pummeling them 10-1 and 13-7 in the first two games of an American League Division Series they won in four. Then they lost the first two AL Championship Series games at home to Seattle, and came back to win in seven, which says there's some grit there, too.

And this is a team that was second in baseball only to Kansas City in not striking out during the regular season, fanning only 1,099 times, facing a Dodgers pitching staff that led the majors in striking people out (1,505).

Maybe that Blue Jays flexibility was the main factor Friday night. Blake Snell, dominant in his three previous starts this postseason – an 0.86 ERA, 28 strikeouts, five walks and six hits in 21 innings, including one hit and 10 strikeouts over eight innings in Game 1 against Milwaukee – struggled from the start.

He only struck out three, two of those on back-to-back two-strike foul tips by Myles Straw and Andres Gimenez in the second inning, and Toronto had him under stress from the beginning. Snell had to throw 29 pitches to get out of a bases-loaded situation in the first, gave up four hits in the first three innings and served up a first-pitch, four-seam fastball – a juicy one – that Daulton Varsho hit off the batter's eye in center field for a two-run homer to tie the score in the fourth.

Snell was the losing pitcher – his first loss in four decisions this postseason – because reliever Emmet Sheehan, pitching in his first World Series game and appearing flustered amid the din of the Toronto faithful, started the nine-run conflagration in the sixth by allowing three inherited runners to score on two hits and a bases-loaded walk. Anthony Banda then punctuated it, serving up a letter-high, middle-of-the-plate slider that Barger hit into the right field bleachers for a 9-2 lead and a place in World Series history.

Alejandro Kirk's two-run shot made it 11-2 later in that inning. Shohei Ohtani's two-run homer in the seventh, his sixth of the playoffs, was but a slight whimper of protest.

So what now? When a questioner suggested in the postgame interview room that the Jays were a different-looking team than the Dodgers were used to, Roberts said, "You know, actually, they're a lot as far as putting the ball in play like the (Milwaukee) Brewers."

Judging by recent performance, the Blue Jays do it much better.

"When he (Snell) had count leverage, he really couldn't put 'em away because they were putting the ball in play," Roberts said. "And there were just a couple bad walks in there. But you got to give those guys credit. They certainly fought."

Friday night's performances of Sheehan and Banda weren't exactly reason for optimism with a group of relief pitchers who might be about to face another stress test. A question mark for much of the last three months of the regular season but more efficient recently, the bullpen underwent another change when Alex Vesia left the team to be with his wife because of what the team has referred to as a "deeply personal family matter."

Obviously it's serious enough for Roberts to say before the game that "unless something unforeseen happens," the most likely scenario was that Vesia wouldn't be available for the Series.

"We just didn't want to have any potential for any kind of pressure," Dodgers president of baseball operations Andrew Friedman said before the game. "This is so much bigger than baseball. For us, it was doing whatever small part we could to just a hundred percent be supportive."

That's admirable, obviously. Family is and should always be number one. But Vesia's absence leaves a hole, and asking Edgardo Henriquez and Will Klein to fill it might be asking too much.

So maybe the solution will ultimately lie with the offense. The Dodgers wasted opportunities in the second and third innings to put pressure on Trey Yesavage, the 22-year-old who began this season in Class A and was the second-youngest Game 1 starter in World Series history. (Only Brooklyn's Ralph Branca in 1947 was younger.)

The Dodgers had the bases loaded with one out and a run in but couldn't get any more in the second inning, stranded a runner at second in the third inning and didn't have another runner in scoring position all evening.

"Even (when) you look back at last couple of weeks, there's some pivotal at-bats that can flip games. I think that we can be better at that," Roberts said. "At times, I think that the offense looks great as far as building innings, but there's some key at-bats that you got to win pitches and use the other side of the field, get a hit, take a walk, whatever it might be.

"We can be better. We need to be better. (Toronto Game 2 starter Kevin) Gausman, these guys are fired up. They're playing good baseball. So just one through nine, we just got to continue to take good at-bats and play good baseball and then we'll be fine."

If you're a Dodger fan, you don't want to even think of the alternative. ■

WORLD SERIES GAME 2
October 25, 2025 | Toronto, Ontario
DODGERS 5, BLUE JAYS 1

A Complete Statement

Yoshinobu Yamamoto Pitches His Second Consecutive Complete Game to Even World Series

By Bill Plunkett

Caulk and weather stripping are good ways to weather-proof your house in these parts. Yoshinobu Yamamoto is the best way the Dodgers have found to bullpen-proof a game.

Yamamoto pitched his second consecutive complete game of the postseason, holding a Toronto Blue Jays lineup that scored 11 runs in Game 1 to just one run on four hits as the Dodgers won Game 2 of the World Series, 5-1, on Saturday night and sent the best-of-seven series to Los Angeles even at one game apiece.

Game 3 is Monday, with Tyler Glasnow scheduled to start for the Dodgers and Max Scherzer for the Blue Jays.

"It's amazing," Dodgers first baseman Freddie Freeman said of Yamamoto's back-to-back complete games. "There's not enough adjectives, superlatives, anything you wanna say. To do it in back-to-back starts, in what? Less than 110 pitches (105)?"

Yamamoto finished Saturday's game by retiring 20 consecutive Blue Jays batters in the first World Series complete game since Kansas City's Johnny Cueto did it against the New York Mets in Game 2 in 2015.

"Didn't know it was 20, so that's pretty cool, too," Dodgers pitching coach Mark Prior said.

No pitcher had thrown consecutive complete games in the postseason since Arizona Diamondbacks ace Curt Schilling, who tossed three in a row in the 2001 National League Division Series and NLCS. No Dodgers pitcher had done it since Orel Hershiser in the 1988 World Series.

"To be honest, I'm not sure about the history, but I'm very happy about what I did today," Yamamoto said through his interpreter.

No one was happier than Dodgers manager Dave Roberts, who was able to spend the entire game seated comfortably in the dugout and not trudging out to the mound to make a pitching change with his fingers crossed.

"Outstanding, uber competitive, special," Roberts said. "He was just locked in tonight. It was one of those things – he said before the series, losing is not an option, and he had that look tonight."

Not right away.

The first batter reached base in each of the first three innings against Yamamoto. He had to work out of a first-and-third jam with no outs in the first inning. He struck out Vladimir Guerrero Jr., got Alejandro Kirk on a soft liner to first base and froze Daulton Varsho with a full-count curveball for a called strike three.

It took 23 pitches for him to get through the first inning. No one was thinking about a complete game then.

Yoshinobu went the distance, holding the Blue Jays to just one run on four hits as the Dodgers took Game 2 to even the series. (AP Images)

LA
Dodgers
18
World Series
FERNANDO
34

"After that first inning, I was thinking six," said Roberts, who couldn't have felt good about making his next call to the bullpen after Game 1's nine-run explosion. "I felt he would find a way to get through six. It's an aggressive swinging team. I thought the stuff was good, so I felt that he could manage to get through six. Then the pitch count kind of stayed where it needed to stay. And then for me, I just didn't see anything fall off as far as his delivery and the execution."

In the third inning, though, he hit George Springer with a pitch to start the inning then gave up a line drive off the wall in left field by Guerrero. Guerrero was held to a single but Springer went to third on the hit and scored on a sacrifice fly by Kirk to tie the score.

That was the first of the 20 Blue Jays retired in order by Yamamoto. An even more important number – he was able to do it on just 79 pitches through seven innings, keeping the Dodgers' flame-throwing (not that way) bullpen quiet.

"I mean, his heartbeat – honestly, he's in control the whole time," Prior said. "I said it last time with Milwaukee (Yamamoto's complete-game win in Game 2 of the NLCS), he gave up the first-pitch home run – settled in, never seemed flustered, never seemed rattled by it. Just kept making pitches, going pitch-to-pitch.

"Same thing tonight. He made two really good pitches to get 0-2 on Springer in the first at-bat, tried to elevate one more time. Springer obviously put a good swing on it. It was midline. And then he makes another really good pitch to Lukes and gives up the flare. Just kept making pitches. We've seen that in the past from him. But he's just really determined to stay disciplined to his process, and really just unwavering. Just, 'I'm gonna make a pitch and I'm gonna execute,' and he's gonna gather the information and go on to the next pitch. And from then on, he was in pretty much control the whole time. His emotional, heartbeat, however you want to say, just doesn't seem fazed. And given the situation, given the magnitude of these games, given what we were coming off of last night, it's remarkable. It really is. Really impressive."

Game 1 made offensive history – the first pinch-hit grand slam in World Series history and the biggest single inning (the Blue Jays' nine-run sixth inning) in a World Series game since 1968. The Game 2 starters – Yamamoto and Kevin Gausman – just made offense history for most of the night.

The Dodgers got on the board in the first inning with the kind of at-bats they've been hoping to see more often. Freeman fouled off three pitches at 2-and-2 before lashing a double into the right-field corner. Smith followed with a two-out RBI single.

They didn't see any more of those kind of at-bats for a long time. Gausman retired the next 17 Dodgers in order.

"He was pitching really well," Smith said of the Blue Jays' starter. "He was really locating the fastball at the bottom. His split was really on. He threw a few sliders, maybe not as many as we thought. He was just mixing his fastball and splits. Those were tough at-bats."

Smith finally ended Gausman's run when he got a 3-and-2 fastball on the inner half and crushed it, sending it 404 feet down the left field line for a solo home run. Two batters later, Muncy got a 2-and-2 fastball on the outside corner and sent it in the same direction for an opposite-field homer (his fourth in 21 career at-bats against Gausman).

The Dodgers' offense did what it could to make Yamamoto even more comfortable with two more runs in the eighth on singles by Andy Pages and Shohei Ohtani, a run-scoring wild pitch and Smith's third RBI of the night when he hit into a force out but beat out the double-play attempt.

After that 23-pitch first inning, Yamamoto threw more than a dozen pitches in an inning just twice more – during the Blue Jays' one-run third inning (13) and while striking out the side in the eighth.

Max Muncy receives a sunflower seed shower after homering in the seventh inning of Game 2 to give the Dodgers a 3-1 lead. (AP Images)

Roki Sasaki briefly got up in the Dodgers' bullpen but there was no debate about letting Yamamoto finish what he started.

"There was no discussion," Prior said. "We talk every inning. Probably from the sixth inning on it was more like, 'All good?' It was a very simple question. 'Yes,' and then we just move on."

Yamamoto struck out eight and walked none, relying on his splitter (34 of his 105 pitches) but also getting five of his 17 swing-and-misses with his curveball.

"It was his night. He executed every pitch," Guerrero said.

Yamamoto has emerged as a big-time postseason performer. The Dodgers have won seven of his eight postseason starts since he joined the team last year.

"As he was going along in the fifth, sixth, seventh inning, I was just trying to think about how poised and in control of the game, what he's trying to do," Freeman said. "It's four or five pitches and it feels like he could hit a flea with it. He can throw it wherever he wants. Sets up hitters. Understands hitters' swings. He's just incredible. We saw it last year when he came back from injury. He was doing it in the postseason then, too. Just stayed healthy all year (in 2025). So you get to see it a little bit more." ■

WORLD SERIES GAME 3
October 27, 2025 | Los Angeles, California
DODGERS 6, BLUE JAYS 5 (F/18)

Marathon Men

Freddie Freeman's Walk-Off Homer Lifts Dodgers to 18-Inning Win in World Series Game 3

By Bill Plunkett

Shohei Ohtani had one of the best games in World Series history – and that wasn't even the half of it. Literally – the Toronto Blue Jays didn't let him swing after the seventh inning.

It took an epic World Series game jam-packed with so much drama and so many momentum changes early that it spilled over into extra innings – and just kept going – to contain Ohtani's latest feats of strength. With Ohtani seemingly ready for a mid-game promotion to some higher league, the Dodgers finally won Game 3 on Monday night, 6-5, on Freddie Freeman's walk-off home run in the 18th inning to take a two games to one lead in the best-of-seven series.

The game tied Game 3 of the 2018 World Series between the Dodgers and Boston Red Sox as the longest game in World Series history (innings-wise). That one ended on a walk-off home run by Max Muncy.

"As it started going on, it was starting to feel like deja vu for me," Muncy said. "I hit the home run just foul (during his 14th inning at-bat Monday). It just was really starting to feel like deja vu."

It was the first World Series game to end on a walk-off hit since ... Freeman's grand slam in the 10th inning of Game 1 against the New York Yankees last year.

"That's what you're talking about as kids," Freeman said. "It was always bases loaded, you know, and two outs, bottom of the ninth. I know it happened in the 10th (last year). But to have it happen again a year later, to hit another walk-off, it's kind of amazing, crazy, and I'm just glad we won and we're up 2-1, and we got our Shohei on the mound tomorrow."

There was a seventh-inning stretch – and a 14th-inning stretch. Stadium organist Dieter Ruehle, who plays the theme from "Gilligan's Island" whenever a game reaches the 3-hour mark ("a 3-hour cruise") got to play it twice as 605 pitches were thrown over 6 hours and 39 minutes.

"It's one of the greatest World Series games of all time," Dodgers manager Dave Roberts said. "I'm spent emotionally."

After Blake Treinen gave up a run on three consecutive hits in the seventh inning, six Dodgers relievers – Jack Dreyer, Roki Sasaki, Emmet Sheehan, Clayton Kershaw, Edgardo Henriquez and Will Klein – pitched 11 scoreless innings. Roberts used 10 pitchers in all, leaving just Blake Snell, Yoshinobu Yamamoto and Ohtani as the only ones not called upon. Yamamoto volunteered to pitch and was warming up as Klein – who hadn't pitched in a game in a month and never more than two innings in any MLB game – persevered through a fourth inning of relief in the 18th.

"Probably college. My junior year when I was still a starter," Klein said of the last time he had thrown 72 pitches in a game as he did Monday. "I realized that

Freddie Freeman's walk-off home run in the 18th inning ended Game 3 after 6 hours and 39 minutes. (Los Angeles Daily News: Keith Birmingham)

when I looked around in the bullpen and my name was the only one still there. ... I was just going to go until I couldn't, and that's kind of what happened and, thankfully, Freddie saved us from Yamamoto having to do the same thing.

"Yamamoto throwing out of the 'pen on one day rest after nine innings (in Game 2) would have been insane."

Almost as crazy as someone reaching base nine times in a game – and starting the next one on the mound about 18 hours later.

Game 4 – or does it count as Game 5 now? – is scheduled for Tuesday at 5 p.m. with Ohtani and Shane Bieber expected to pitch – yeah, he does that too.

"I want to go to sleep as soon as possible so I will be ready," Ohtani said through his interpreter in the on-field interview.

Ohtani focused on his day job Monday and ripped off four extra-base hits – two doubles and two home runs – in his first four at-bats. After that, the Blue Jays took the bat out of his hand, intentionally walking him three times with no one on base, once with a runner on third (in the 13th inning) and once more unintentionally (on four pitches nowhere near the strike zone in the 17th inning). Ohtani is the first player in history to reach base nine times in a World Series game – and the first to be intentionally walked four times in any postseason game.

Instead of holding up four fingers to signal an intentional walk, the Blue Jays might just hold up a calendar turned to November, signaling their intention not to pitch to him again in this series. In the past two games played at Dodger Stadium (Game 4 of the National League Championship Series against the Milwaukee Brewers and Game 3 of this World Series), Ohtani has gone 7 for 7 with six walks, five home runs and two doubles. Oh, yeah – he also pitched six scoreless innings and struck out 10 in between some of those at-bats.

"He's arguably the best player on the planet, you know," Blue Jays manager John Schneider said. "They have a really talented lineup. It's not the easiest thing in the world to just walk him and face Mookie (Betts) and Freddie."

Betts thought it over but couldn't agree.

"Oh, I would too," said Betts, who was 1 for 4 after all those walks. "I would too – especially the way I've been swinging it. So I need to figure something out so they – naw, they're still going to walk him. It doesn't matter."

Ohtani's first double Monday went for naught when his teammates left him stranded in the first inning. The home run came in the third inning and made it 2-0 after Teoscar Hernandez had also gone deep in the second against Blue Jays starter Max Scherzer. That prompted a vigorous bat toss from Hernandez, who had just one hit and nine strikeouts in his previous 14 at-bats this postseason and was dropped a spot in the Game 3 lineup.

Dodgers starter Tyler Glasnow needed some help to keep the Blue Jays scoreless through three innings. After a leadoff single by Bo Bichette, Daulton Varsho took a 3-and-0 pitch from Glasnow clearly above the strike zone and started to head to first base. But home plate umpire Mark Wegner called it a strike – eventually.

The delayed call brought Varsho back to the batter's box but a confused Bichette kept walking away from first base. Glasnow threw to Freeman who tagged the bemused Bichette out.

Glasnow didn't get any help in the fourth inning. After walking the leadoff hitter, he got Bichette to hit a ground ball to Tommy Edman's left, possibly a double-play ball. Edman misplayed it and runners were at the corners with no outs.

Varsho flew out to shallow left field but Glasnow hung a first-pitch curveball to Alejandro Kirk, who sent it over the wall in left-center for a three-run home run. Two more singles and a sacrifice fly made it a four-run inning for the Blue Jays and a 4-2 lead.

The Dodgers tied it in the fifth. After a leadoff single by Kiké Hernandez, Ohtani shot a line drive off the wall in left-center for his second double of the night. Hernandez scored from first base and Freeman drove Ohtani in when he hooked a single past Vladimir Guerrero Jr. at first base.

Guerrero showed off a different skill to give the Blue Jays another lead in the seventh. He singled

Dodgers players wait to mob Freddie Freeman at home plate after Freeman's home run sealed the Dodgers' 6-5 win in Game 3. (Los Angeles Daily News: Keith Birmingham)

with two outs then – after three false starts, running on pitches Bichette fouled off – he scored from first base when Bichette singled down the line and the ball took an odd carom off the side wall (or possibly the ball boy's chair).

Ohtani matched that in the bottom of the seventh with his second home run of the game and eighth of the postseason, tying Corey Seager (2020) for the franchise record – on the first pitch after Blue Jays pitching coach Pete Walker went out to the mound to discuss with reliever Seranthony Dominguez how to pitch to Ohtani. One assumes he did not suggest the center-cut fastball that Ohtani sent 401 feet into the pavilion in left-center.

The parade of zeroes began after that. The Dodgers got 1⅔ innings from Roki Sasaki, the first scoreless relief outing of the postseason from Emmet Sheehan (2⅔ innings), two redeeming defensive plays by Edman – throwing a runner out at third in the ninth inning and home in the 10th – and one out (of the 105 recorded in the game) from Clayton Kershaw to end the top of the 12th inning with the bases loaded.

Klein entered in the 15th and Roberts said on the broadcast that he wouldn't go past the 17th inning – even if it meant sending a position player into the game. But Klein kept going and was mobbed by teammates after Freeman's home run.

"That was so cool," Klein said. "I never dreamed that anything like this would happen. So just having the guys like Kersh, Freddie, Shohei, Mookie, all those guys like kind of celebrating me for a second there was just insane. I don't think I could have dreamt a dream that good." ■

G.O.A.T. Status

Soak it Up, Shohei Ohtani Keeps Making History

By Mirjam Swanson | October 27, 2025

What do you say about the game that has everything? History and high drama so good it needed a record-tying extra nine innings and 6 hours, 39 minutes to sort itself out.

There were heroes aplenty and there was the G.O.A.T. – lots of him. Shohei Ohtani, greatest of all time, all over the bases, all game long.

Game 4's starting pitcher continued to set all kinds of history at the plate in Game 3 on Monday, helping the Dodgers secure an 18-inning, 6-5 victory to take a 2-1 lead in their World Series matchup with the Toronto Blue Jays.

Next Ohtani will pitch – and hit, if the Blue Jays are brave enough to pitch to him – as the Dodgers continue their quest Tuesday for a second consecutive world championship and their third since 2020.

On Monday, Ohtani had already raked two home runs and two doubles by the time Toronto intentionally walked him with one out in the ninth inning, and then again with two out in the 11th and in the 13th. The free pass in the ninth would normally have been unthinkable, this time of year. But this time it was an obvious move; duh, it would be dumb to let him rip another extra-base hit off of another of your pitchers.

Truly, Toronto probably ought to have walked Ohtani in the seventh, before he squared the game, 5-5, with a 401-foot home run to left field off righty Seranthony Dominguez.

But the Blue Jays didn't.

"We were trying to pitch around him," Manager John Schneider said, "... after that you just kind of take the bat out of his hands."

So Ohtani's fourth extra-base hit tied the score and tied him for the most in a World Series game. Only Frank Isbell had as many, back in ... 1906. Isbell's four doubles in Game 5 lifted the Chicago White Sox to an 8-6 victory over the Chicago Cubs.

Ohtani's 12 total bases also go down as a Dodgers' World Series record – and his seventh and eighth postseason home runs tied him for the most in franchise history. Also, his reaching base nine times? Three more than any other player in any other World Series game – and tied for the record for any MLB game.

His was also just the fifth multi-homer game in Dodgers' World Series history – and his third, personally, of these playoffs.

Stop a second and savor that. Soak it in. You'll be telling his story for a long time.

Because this man is worth the price of admission – and the $80 parking fee too.

"There's no more adjectives you can describe Shohei, a once-in-a-10-generational player," said Freddie Freeman, Monday's final hero for homering in the 18th to end the contest that tied the Dodgers' previous record for longest World Series game.

"He's a freak," said reliever Will Klein, the 10th Dodgers pitcher who threw a career-high four scoreless innings for the win. "Being on a team with him is a great honor."

And when Ohtani takes the mound Tuesday, he'll be chasing probably the greatest big league baseball game of all time – his three-home run, 10-strikeout hitting/pitching night in the Dodgers' closeout victory in a National League Championship Series sweep over the Milwaukee Brewers on Oct. 17.

Put together, Ohtani's past two games at Dodger Stadium look like this: Home run, walk, home run, home run, double, home run, double, home run,

Shohei Ohtani reached base a record nine times in the Dodgers' 18-inning Game 3 win. (Los Angeles Daily News: Keith Birmingham)

walk, walk, walk, walk, walk – the first four of the final five walks were all intentional passes, which, naturally, set an MLB record.

Jordanesque. Tiger Mania-manic-ificent. Just silly. A super-duper-star at his most superb.

But go ahead, jilted Jays fans, tell yourselves you don't need him.

That's how the nice Canadian fans serenaded Ohtani – who seriously considered leaving the Angels for Toronto in free agency a couple of years ago before opting instead for Dodger Blue – with a "We Don't Need You!" chant during the Dodgers' Game 1 loss in Toronto.

Ohtani laughed it off, of course, because they were being silly too.

Because who couldn't use a unicorn who's making a habit of providing answers to questions we'd never even thought about asking, like: Was that the greatest single baseball game ever by a single player?

Who wouldn't rather have this phenom on their side than the other side?

Who wouldn't appreciate everything the pride of Oshu, Japan, has brought to our city, and to Southern California. Ohtani is a do-everything talent, who does it all with a smile – and with the occasional, satisfying bat flip.

He will take the mound Tuesday for his first World Series start after making his debut in the Fall Classic last year as solely a hitter, because he was still recovering from 2023 surgery to repair the ulnar collateral ligament in his right elbow.

Since picking pitching back up this June 16, Ohtani started 14 games and posted a 2.87 ERA.

In his first postseason pitching appearance, Ohtani got the win in Game 1 of the NLDS against the Philadelphia Phillies. And then came Game 4 against the Brewers, his first 100-pitch performance since returning from surgery – and just his latest start before Game 4 on Tuesday, whatever mind-bending history he's got in store for us then.

"He was on base eight or nine times tonight, running the bases," Roberts said, "... [and] he's taking the mound tomorrow. He'll be ready."

"I want," Ohtani said on the Fox broadcast, "to go to sleep as soon as possible." ■

WORLD SERIES GAME 4
October 28, 2025 | Los Angeles, California
BLUE JAYS 6, DODGERS 2

Wake-Up Call

Blue Jays Get to Shohei Ohtani, Beat Dodgers in Game 4 to Even World Series

By Bill Plunkett

The Hangover IV.

Like that exhausted franchise, the Dodgers and Toronto Blue Jays returned to the stage with less energy and enthusiasm for their parts, fatigued from the historic drama of Game 3 on Monday night.

Not even the pregame screeching of Ken Jeong or the flexing of Flea could shock much life into Game 4 on Tuesday. Prince Harry and Meghan would be forgiven if they thought they had stumbled into a weekend series in July, not the Fall Classic.

The biggest jolt of excitement came in the third inning when Vladimir Guerrero Jr. hit a two-run home run off Shohei Ohtani that put the Blue Jays in front to stay. Another crooked number against the Dodgers' bullpen in the seventh inning cemented a 6-2 Game 4 victory that evened the World Series at two games apiece.

Game 5 is a rematch of the Game 1 starting pitchers – Blake Snell for the Dodgers, rookie right-hander Trey Yesavage for the Blue Jays. This championship will be decided north of the border in Game 6 or 7.

"It's a series. That's why you play seven games," Dodgers shortstop Mookie Betts said. "Like I said before, they're not in the World Series by luck. They're a really good ballclub."

The Dodgers weren't very good in July – and they weren't very good in this sequel. Both their tepid offense and the warm weather recalled those days.

They scratched out a run in the second inning against Blue Jays starter Shane Bieber. Max Muncy worked a one-out walk, went to third on a single by Tommy Edman and scored on a sacrifice fly by Kiké Hernandez.

That was all the productivity they could manage returning to work after a late night of partying.

They had just four hits in the first seven innings and didn't get another runner to second base until the sixth inning, giving fans no use for their rally towels other than wiping the mustard from their lips.

"You know, I don't know," Dodgers manager Dave Roberts said when asked if fatigue from the 18-inning marathon in Game 3 was a factor in the lack of offense. "I think that you got to give credit to (Blue Jays starter Shane) Bieber for making pitches, getting ahead. Those guys ... went through the same thing as we did. I felt like we were prepared tonight. Guys came in fresh. Starting off with the (outstanding defensive) play from Kiké (Hernandez) in left field. I thought we had some good kind of energy early, and then it just kind of petered out a little bit."

Betts wouldn't blame the after-effects of a late night for the lack of offense.

"No. It's not our first time scoring two," he said. "So no, it has nothing to do with it. It's a World Series, and if you can't get up for a World Series, then you need to find something else."

He's right – it is not the Dodgers' first sub-par offensive showing this postseason. Since scoring 18 runs in their two-game dismissal of the Cincinnati Reds in the Wild Card Series, the Dodgers have averaged 3.75 runs per game. They've struggled especially in the clutch, batting .183 (17 for 93) with runners in scoring position since the National League Division Series.

"We haven't found our rhythm. We haven't," Roberts said. "It sort of draws dead at certain parts of the lineup and different parts, different innings, different games. Guys are competing. Certainly, in the postseason, you're seeing everyone's best."

Roberts said he will "think long and hard" about some lineup changes for Game 5. He pinch hit for Andy Pages in the seventh inning Tuesday. Pages is just 4 for 50 this postseason. Tommy Edman played center field for five innings in Game 3 and could be an option there now.

"It might look a little bit different tomorrow," Roberts said.

"I've got to make a decision. Essentially, am I going to play Andy, am I going to play (Alex) Call, or am I going to play Miggy Ro? So just kind of trying to think through all that stuff and net it out and see what gives us the best chance tomorrow."

After reaching base nine times in Game 3 – including walks in his last five plate appearances – Ohtani walked to lead off the first inning for the Dodgers. That extended his World Series record to 11 consecutive plate appearances in which he reached base (starting with an eighth-inning single in Game 2). But it ended there, Ohtani was 0 for 3 with two strikeouts the rest of the way.

"We're facing quality arms this time of the year against really good teams, and we're facing the best of the best, so I think it's not that easy," Ohtani said through his interpreter. "But at the same time, we could do at least the bare minimum to be able to put up some runs."

On the mound, he showed some of the effects of all that walking – and running – in Game 3. His fastball velocity was down slightly, from fatigue or a strategic attempt to extend his resources. He relied more on his sweeper and curveball.

Even superheroes make mistakes – come on, Superman went to work for a newspaper – and Ohtani made his when he hung a sweeper to Guerrero for the two-run home run.

"That swing was huge," Blue Jays manager John Schneider said. "A sweeper is a pitch designed to generate pop-ups, in my opinion, and the swing that Vlad put on it was elite. After last night and kind of all the recognition that went into Shohei individually and he's on the mound today, it's a huge swing from Vlad. It's a huge swing to get us going."

Ohtani did get into the seventh inning for a pitching staff stretched thin by Tuesday's doubleheader-in-one Game 3. When he gave up a leadoff single to Daulton Varsho and a double off the wall to Ernie Clement in the seventh, Ohtani's time on the mound was over.

"I thought he looked really good tonight," Dodgers catcher Will Smith said. "He made the one mistake to Vlad, a backup slider he hit the home run off of. Just that last inning they got a couple hits. It happens. We weren't able to minimize that."

After their heroic effort in Game 3 – six relievers held the Blue Jays scoreless for the final 11 innings of the 18-inning marathon – the Dodgers' bullpen went back to their troublesome ways.

Anthony Banda gave up an RBI single to Andres Gimenez but seemed to be headed for an escape when Muncy handled Isiah Kiner-Falefa's line drive and fired across the diamond to get Gimenez for a double play.

The play at first was close, though, and replay review overturned the call. That opened the door for another run to score on a ground out and two more on back-to-back RBI singles by Bo Bichette and Addison Barger after Blake Treinen entered the game.

The Dodgers managed a second run in the ninth inning with a Max Muncy double in the mix.

"They're executing really well right now," Muncy said. "We're not taking advantage of the few mistakes that they're making. Like I said, they're just executing. Anytime a pitcher executes, it's gonna be a tough day.

"(The offense has been) not great. We're missing on the big opportunities, myself included. I'm one of the big culprits of that. I've had some opportunities and I haven't cashed in. We gotta get the big hit." ■

WORLD SERIES GAME 5

October 29, 2025 | Los Angeles, California

BLUE JAYS 6, DODGERS 1

Backs Against the Wall

Dodgers' Offense Goes Silent Against Rookie as Blue Jays Take 3-2 Series Lead

By Bill Plunkett

If the Toronto Blue Jays claim a World Series title this weekend, Trey Yesavage will never have to pay for another Timbit in his life.

A starting pitcher stepped up to dominate Game 5 and tip the World Series in his team's favor. But it was not the one with two Cy Young Awards. It was the one who started this season pitching in the Class-A Florida State League for the Dunedin Blue Jays.

Yesavage, a rookie right-hander, struck out 12 Dodgers and allowed just three hits in seven innings as the Toronto Blue Jays won Game 5, 6-1, on Wednesday night and took a three-games-to-two advantage in the World Series.

"We trust each other. We believe we're the best team in baseball," Dodgers catcher Will Smith said. "We've had our backs against the wall a lot this year. Fighting through injuries, fighting through expectations and all that. This is a tough group, and I got no problem going in there and winning two games, and we'll be ready for that."

After splitting the first two games in Toronto, the Dodgers lost two of three at home. If the defending champions are going to go back-to-back, they will indeed have to win back-to-back games in Toronto. Game 6 is Friday night with Game 2 hero Yoshinobu Yamamoto scheduled to pitch for the Dodgers.

Game 6 will be the first time the Dodgers have faced elimination since Game 4 of the National League Division Series last fall.

"We faced this last year. We were down 2-1 to the Padres and won two games in a row. We can do it again," first baseman Freddie Freeman said.

"We feel very good about our pitching and our pitching staff. We're going to need Yoshi to do it again and hopefully as an offense we can score some runs for him."

That has become harder to do the deeper the Dodgers have gotten into October.

Game 5 was the fifth time in the past 11 postseason games that the Dodgers managed just two runs or less. Since scoring 18 runs in their two-game dismissal of the Cincinnati Reds in the Wild Card Series, the Dodgers have averaged just 3.5 runs per game over their next 13 postseason games. They have scored just four in their past 29 innings against a Blue Jays team that got here on the strength of its hitting, not its pitching.

"It seems like at-bats are snowballing on us right now," said Dodgers outfielder Kiké Hernandez, whose home run in the third inning produced the Dodgers' only run of Game 5. "We're getting pitches to hit, we're missing them, and we're expanding the (strike) zone with two strikes. I think the best thing that can happen for us is a day off. Get a day to regroup and figure it out. As a group, it's time for us to show our character and put up a fight and see what happens."

Yesavage's 12 strikeouts in Game 5 are the most ever by a rookie pitcher in the World Series, topping Brooklyn Dodger Don Newcombe's 11 in Game 1 of the 1949 World Series.

Yesavage made $57,204 in MLB this season – the pro-rated portion of the major-league minimum after he was promoted in September. But he dominated a Dodgers' lineup that made more than $148 million. That lineup seems to have started its winter hibernation early – and threatens to take the down the team's hopes for a repeat championship.

"It doesn't feel great," Dodgers manager Dave Roberts said. "You clearly see those guys finding ways to get hits, move the baseball forward, and we're not doing a good job of it. I thought Yesavage was good tonight mixing his fastball, slider, and the split. But, yeah, you still have to use the whole field and take what they give you, and if they're not going to allow for slug, then you've got to be able to kind of redirect and club down to take competitive at-bats. ... Those guys are doing it.

"We have that ability. We've got to make some adjustments."

The 20th pick in last year's draft, Yesavage raced through the Blue Jays' system to make his major-league debut in September. He has been a postseason revelation, striking out 39 in 26 innings over five postseason starts.

"When you go into a game like this, you attack a lane and our lane against Yesavage was up," Freeman said. "It was just a complete 180 from Game 1 (when Yesavage lasted just four innings). His command was pinpoint tonight. We were fighting that lane and he was still getting his slider and splitter down in the zone for strikes. That was the difference from Game 1. He had a lot of non-competitive misses in Game 1. Today he didn't have that."

The 6-foot-4 right-hander's unusually high release point and an exceptional splitter have been the main drivers of his success in October. But the Dodgers were able to lay off the pitch. They swung at just 10 of the 30 he threw.

It was his slider that proved devastating. He got 14 of his 23 swings-and-misses with that pitch, throwing it more often than either his splitter or fastball.

"Strikes," Kiké Hernandez said, identifying Yesavage's most effective pitch. "His slider was really good tonight. I think his slider was his difference-maker. It was harder and tighter than it was in Toronto. We weren't really able to pick it up, and his split is pretty good. Just seemed like we were – I don't know if we were in between kind of. Kudos to him. We've just got to be better."

Yesavage retired the first seven Dodgers in order, the last five on consecutive strikeouts before Kiké Hernandez drove a high fastball into the left-field pavilion for a solo home run. The Dodgers' only other hits off the rookie were infield singles by Teoscar Hernandez in the fourth and seventh innings.

Teoscar Hernandez said Yesavage looked like "a different pitcher" than the one the Dodgers faced in Game 1.

"He located every pitch he wanted to today," Dodgers third baseman Max Muncy said. "Game 1 he didn't necessarily have the best command, and today, I don't think he missed a single spot, with the exception of down below the zone, which is what he wants to do. He didn't give us anything to take advantage of."

The lack of offense required a shutout from Dodgers starter Blake Snell. That possibility disappeared on the game's first pitch.

Davis Schneider hit the first one for a leadoff home run. Vladimir Guerrero Jr. sent Snell's third pitch of the game into the left-field pavilion as well. It was the first time a World Series game started with back-to-back home runs.

Snell wasn't bad after that. He got touched for another run in the fourth inning thanks to the latest entry on Teoscar Hernandez's highlight-reel of poor defense.

Criticized during the regular season for his occasional lapses in effort on defense, Teoscar Hernandez overcompensated on Daulton Varsho's pop-up near the right field line. Hernandez made an ill-conceived – and poorly executed – sliding attempt, turning Varsho's hit into a triple. The Blue Jays cashed it in immediately with a sacrifice fly by Ernie Clement.

Roberts came to get Snell after 116 pitches with Guerrero coming up again in the seventh. And the Blue Jays romped like kids turned loose in a ball pit when they got into the Dodgers' bullpen.

Edgardo Henriquez walked Guerrero, yanking ball four so far wide of the plate it went past catcher Will Smith to the backstop. Henriquez didn't retire any of the three batters he faced, sandwiching two walks around an RBI single by Bo Bichette.

Anthony Banda shut down that inning but gave up another run in the eighth.

"We've got a lot of confidence in him," shortstop Mookie Betts said of Game 6 starter Yamamoto. "But we've got to hit. We've got to hit. Yoshi is going to do his thing. We need him to, obviously. But we've got to hit. There's no way around that." ■

WORLD SERIES GAME 6

October 31, 2025 | Toronto, Ontario

DODGERS 3, BLUE JAYS 1

Night of the Living Dead

Dodgers Find New Life with Halloween Win, Force Decisive Game 7

By Bill Plunkett

Spanning the globe from Tokyo to Toronto and the calendar from March to November, one game will determine how these Dodgers will be remembered – as the first team in a quarter-century to repeat as champions ... or as expensive disappointments who failed to live up to the demands of their outsized expectations.

Clinging to an early lead by their fingertips and white-knuckling through an unexpected nine clutch outs from their bullpen – ending with a game-saving defensive play by Kiké Hernandez – the Dodgers kept their season alive, beating the Toronto Blue Jays, 3-1, in Game 6 on Friday night, forcing a Game 7 to decide the World Series on Saturday night.

"Pretty epic ending there," Dodgers second baseman Miguel Rojas said.

Even by World Series standards, that was true.

The Dodgers took a 3-1 lead into the ninth inning with Roki Sasaki pitching his second inning. But Sasaki hit Alejandro Kirk with a pitch and gave up a line drive to the center-field wall by Addison Barger – that stuck in the base of the wall.

Defensive replacement Justin Dean pulled up to play the ball off the wall but Hernandez, racing over from left field, threw up his hands. The left-field umpire saw that and the ball wedged in the wall, and ruled a ground-rule double, stopping the runners at second and third.

"I put my hands up right away. I think I put my hands up before him (Dean), and then he put his hands up," Hernandez said. "He put his hands up after I did, and I was just screaming at him to, like, get the ball and throw it in, because that's umpire's discretion. The fact that the ball stuck there doesn't mean that they're actually going to call a ground-rule double. And I was screaming at him, that's kind of why I've lost my voice a little bit. But I was screaming at him to throw it in, and he never did. I'm glad the umpires made the right call."

On came Tyler Glasnow, the presumptive Game 7 starter called upon to get the Dodgers there. He got Ernie Clement to pop out then Andres Gimenez lined a ball to left field. Hernandez charged in to make the catch and threw quickly to second base, doubling Barger off base to end the game – and prompting Mookie Betts to make a leap of relief into Hernandez's arms.

"When he hit the ball, I thought there wasn't a chance, but Kiké took an incredible jump. He could see that the bat broke and he was closing on it," Rojas said. "I don't know if another left fielder makes that play that easily. I think people will see he caught it easily, but that's a difficult ball especially when it breaks off the end of the bat. He's a player who just showed it again, that it doesn't matter what happens, he'll always be prepared."

Starting pitcher Tyler Glasnow came was called upon to close Game 6 and recorded three outs on three pitches while working out of a bases loaded jam. (AP Images)

LA
tional.

It was a fortuitous lull in the roar of the crowd that tipped him off, Hernandez said.

"With Glasnow's stuff, I was anticipating him hitting the ball to the left side of the field," Hernandez said, walking through the game-ending play. "I was playing shallow, tying run on second base, I just wanted to make sure that if he got a hit through the six-hole, I was going to be shallow enough to keep the tying run that was at second base, keep him at third, and the batter runner stay at first.

"But for a split second, as Glasnow threw the ball, the crowd got quiet. I was able to hear that the bat broke, so I just got a really good jump on the ball ... and I felt that the guy on second took a little bit too big of a lead. Off the bat, he might have thought that the ball was gonna drop, so I felt that he was kind of off the bag. But I was coming in full speed, so I didn't want to really throw hard, because I was probably going to throw it over his head. An unbelievable pick by Miggy. I didn't give him the best of throws, but he was able to stay with it.

"And we forced Game 7."

All of that happened faster than Glasnow could follow.

"Dude, I didn't even have enough time to think about it," he said. "I just thought, 'Please don't be a hit. Sweet, it's not a hit. Nice, a double play.' That was my thinking, I guess."

The Dodgers forced a Game 7 despite getting just four hits in the game.

Blue Jays starter Kevin Gausman used his splitter to extend the struggles of the Dodgers' offense. He struck out the side in the first inning, throwing 11 splitters in his 16 pitches. The Dodgers swung eight times, missed seven and fouled off one.

Gausman tied a World Series record with eight strikeouts in the first three innings and got 17 swings-and-misses (most on his splitter), the most in the first three innings of a postseason game since pitch-tracking began in 2008.

Through the first two innings, the Dodgers had produced a total of four runs over a 31-inning stretch. But they bunched three of their hits together to get to Gausman in that third inning.

Tommy Edman got a first-pitch fastball up in the zone and doubled with one out. Blue Jays manager John Schneider made the easy decision to intentionally walk Shohei Ohtani. This time, though, it was Will Smith who followed, not the slumping Betts. Smith went down below the strike zone for a 1-and-0 splitter and doubled into the left-field corner, driving in Edman.

A walk of Freddie Freeman loaded the bases and brought the game to Betts, despite his being dropped two spots in two days. Gausman made a mistake and left a 1-and-2 fastball up to Betts, who singled through the left side, driving in two runs with two outs – his first RBIs of the series.

Ohtani has walked eight times in the World Series, five times intentionally. But that was the first time he scored a run after being walked. The Dodgers didn't have another hit until Ohtani doubled in the eighth inning, though, leaving Yamamoto seemingly as the last man on the wall to protect a 3-1 lead.

The Blue Jays got to him for that one run in the third inning after a leadoff double by Addison Barger. But they didn't get another runner to second base until the sixth when Vladimir Guerrero Jr. doubled with two outs and Bo Bichette walked.

Yamamoto struck out Daulton Varsho with a splitter, his 96th pitch of the night. Yamamoto threw 105 and 111 pitches in his previous two starts (complete-game wins) – and 138 in a complete-game win when his Orix Buffaloes faced this same situation in Game 6 of the 2023 Japan Series.

But 96 was all he threw Friday night.

"Yamamoto did his job for the night, in my opinion," Dodgers manager Dave Roberts said.

"It's never good taking Yamamoto out of a game, certainly in a playoff game. But I think the way that Wrobo's been throwing the baseball, his confidence – it's a different look, and I trust him. I felt he was the right guy for that part of the order."

Calling on his suspect bullpen at this point on Halloween night set up the possibility of a haunting outcome for the Dodgers. But Roberts went to left-hander Justin Wrobleski, who worked around another two-out double to retire the Blue Jays in the seventh.

They put their season in the hands of accidental closer Sasaki next.

Will Smith and the Dodgers didn't flinch up against elimination in Game 6 and set up a deciding Game 7 in Toronto. (AP Images)

He waded through the top of the Blue Jays' order in the eighth, giving up a single to George Springer and walking Guerrero but stranding them both. That took 25 pitches and it was the last outs they would get from Sasaki.

"I just felt that Roki wasn't as sharp, and I just felt we needed some swing-and-miss and Glasnow was the guy," Roberts said. "I had him loose, kind of looming, and then just the situation, I was – the pop-up was huge, but I was looking for somebody that can get some swing-and-miss and some kind of elite stuff and that's why I decided to go with Glasnow."

Glasnow didn't get any swing-and-miss. Known for his October heroics at the plate, Hernandez closed it out with his glove.

"We won. We won the game," Wrobleski said when asked to summarize the drama. "It got a little hairy, got a little weird. But Kiké made a great play. Glas came in and did his thing.

"Game 7."

The Dodgers are now 14-7 in elimination games in 10 seasons with Roberts as manager, including 6-4 on the road.

"We're going to leave it out there," Roberts said. "I don't think that the pressure, the moment isn't going to be too big for us. We got to go out there and win one baseball game. We've done that all year. Everyone's bought in.

"I don't know how the game's going to play out. But as far as kind of the moment, winning a game, I couldn't be more excited to get to sleep and wake up to play a baseball game tomorrow." ■

WORLD SERIES GAME 7
November 1, 2025 | Toronto, Ontario
DODGERS 5, BLUE JAYS 4 (F/11)

Twice as Nice!

Dodgers Win Game 7 in 11 Innings, Become First Repeat World Series Champions in 25 Years

By Bill Plunkett

The weight is over.

They carried it every day from February all the way into November. They were supposed to do this. They were supposed to win. They were supposed to be the first team to repeat as champions since the New York Yankees in 1998-2000. They were supposed to live up to the hyperbolic evaluations that pegged theirs as the most talented roster in baseball history.

It took a game-tying home run in the ninth inning (the first in World Series history) by Miguel Rojas, a game-winning home run by Will Smith in the 11th and 2⅔ innings of relief from Game 6 starter Yoshinobu Yamamoto (Bulldog Mode fully engaged) to make all that come true with a 5-4 victory in Game 7 of the World Series for their third title in six years.

"You dream of those moments, you know, extra innings, put your team ahead – I'll remember that forever," Smith said.

It was a memorable World Series featuring two extra-inning games, shocking momentum shifts and game-saving defensive plays. But the Dodgers didn't always look like the better team in the matchup. The Toronto Blue Jays played better defense overall, took better at-bats consistently and were better in the clutch over the seven games – except when it mattered most.

"That was incredible all the way around," said pitcher Clayton Kershaw, whose career ended as he was warming up in the bullpen. "The Blue Jays are an unbelievable team. They fought so hard and so did we. You saw a lot of guys do things no one would ever ask – starting with Shohei (Ohtani) on short rest and then you have Blake Snell and Tyler Glasnow coming in. I don't think you'll ever see what you saw Yoshi do tonight. That was probably the most gutsy, ballsy thing any guy has ever done. He's used to pitching on a week's rest the whole season. For him to come in and say he's willing to do that and throw not just one inning but – what was it, 2⅔ whatever it was? You can't even describe that."

The Dodgers' first lead in Game 7 didn't come until Smith's home run with two outs in the 11th, the clock past midnight – and the calendar flipped to Nov. 2.

"We didn't lead until we needed to," first baseman Freddie Freeman said with a laugh.

The Dodgers absorbed all of Game 7's setbacks – just as they absorbed the injuries and inconsistencies of a long season to get here – and emerged as champions.

"It's hard to put into words right now. This is amazing. This is about as amazing as it gets," third baseman Max Muncy said. "This is why you play this game. You want to hoist up that trophy. You want to

A veteran presence in the lineup, Miguel Rojas kept the Dodgers' dreams alive with a ninth-inning solo home run that tied the game. (AP Images)

Dodgers
ROJAS
72

spill champagne everywhere. You want to celebrate with your teammates.

"For us, our first game was what March 17? First game was March 17 and the last game was November 1st ... sorry, sorry, fact check me – November 2nd (after midnight). This is why you play this game. You want to hoist up that trophy. This is why you put on a Dodger uniform."

Like almost everything about this season, it didn't go as planned. The Dodgers even found the limits of what Ohtani can do.

It was only the second time in his career Ohtani had started on short rest. He followed a two-inning, rain-shortened start with seven scoreless innings three days later in April 2023 for the Angels.

The circumstances were far different Saturday night, and Ohtani seemed off from the start. He struggled with his command. Only half of his first 30 pitches were strikes. The Blue Jays put the first batter on base in each of the first three innings, putting stress on Ohtani.

He escaped the first two but gave up a three-run home run to Bo Bichette in the third inning.

"They get the three-run bomb early and the roof exploded off this place. Loudest place I think I've ever been," Muncy said. "As a hitting group we kind of met and talked about what we talked about in Philly (at the start of the National League Division Series) – there's going to be a moment where it gets extremely loud. But it's going to be extremely silent when we're on top at the end. That's what we kept thinking about."

Whatever master pitching plan the Dodgers had come up with to cover nine innings, it did not include Ohtani giving up a 110.1 mph laser that traveled 442 feet to straightaway center field for a three-run home run that put their stagnant offense in the trail position.

They wound up using all four of their starting pitchers from this series, plus Emmet Sheehan and Justin Wrobleski (starters by trade moved to the bullpen in the postseason). The one who recorded the most outs – the final eight – was Yamamoto, who threw 96 pitches in Game 6.

"For him to have the same stuff that he had the night before is absolutely mind-blowing to me," Dodgers president of baseball operations Andrew Friedman said. "I got a text (via Will Ireton) last night that Yama was getting treatment to be ready for today. Kind of scoffed at it, like, 'Oh, that's great, he really cares but the likelihood of that is pretty low.' And then today, he got treatment again, and said, 'Hey, I feel really good. Like, I'm able to go out and give at least an inning, and we'll see how my stuff holds.' For him to have the same stuff that he had the night before is really the greatest accomplishment I've ever seen on a Major League Baseball field."

The Dodgers still had to get enough offense to make Yamamoto's heroics pay off.

They got a run in the fourth inning against Jays starter Max Scherzer but stranded two runners after back-to-back outstanding defensive plays by the Blue Jays – diving catches by Daulton Varsho in center field and Guerrero down the first base line.

Both benches – and bullpens – emptied in the fourth inning after Wrobleski hit Gimenez with a pitch, adding some menace to the drama.

The Dodgers crawled within a run in the sixth inning and again on Muncy's solo home run in the eighth.

Rojas finally got the Dodgers even with one out in the ninth inning when he worked the count full against Blue Jays closer Jeff Hoffman then lined a hanging slider over the wall in left field. It was only the second extra-base hit in 21 postseason games for Rojas, the first since another home run for the Miami Marlins in their 2020 NLDS against the Atlanta Braves.

"When you play the game right, treat people right, are the teammate like Miguel is, I think we said it in there (the post-game celebration), the game honors you," Freeman said. "Miguel's been grinding, just doing whatever he could to help this team win. To come up with that moment when you're 36 years old and says

Yoshinobu Yamamoto was an undisputed hero, recording 2⅔ scoreless innings to seal the win just one day after throwing 96 pitches in Game 6. (AP Images)

Dodgers

World Series
Capital One
CONGRAT
CAMPS
Dodgers
2025
Dodgers
2025

he's going to retire after next season, to have that moment in the World Series in Game 7, just absolutely incredible.

"It saved our year."

They escaped a bases-loaded situation in the bottom of the ninth, wasted their own in the top of the 10th and finally took their first lead of the night on Smith's home run with two outs in the 11th.

"A 2-0 count curveball home run? I hope people realize that that's not easy to do," Freeman said. "A lot of us are taking offspeed in that situation. He was on it and hit it out. Like I said, he was the silent assassin a few games ago."

Yamamoto, who threw 96 pitches in the Dodgers' Game 6 win on Friday, ended up throwing 34 pitches to close the clincher. He gave up a leadoff double in the 11th to Vladimir Guerrero Jr., who was sacrificed to third. Addison Barger walked and Alejandro Kirk hit a broken-bat grounder to shortstop Mookie Betts, who started a title-winning double play that ended baseball's 150th major league season, the first that began and ended outside the United States.

Yamamoto won both of them – the first game in Tokyo on March 18 and Game 7 of the World Series. He was named the World Series MVP after getting three of the Dodgers' wins – his complete game in Game 2, six innings in his Game 6 start and the relief win in Game 7.

"You know everybody talks about the Dodgers and how much money we spend and how we're supposed to do this and all that stuff," Kershaw said. "But I tell you what, man – you can't buy the character and the heart and the willingness to do things that other people would not. All the way down our lineup. What Will Smith did – to catch 18 innings, catch a whole game, come up with a big home run. Mookie playing shortstop. Freddie doing what he does. It's all our superstars. There's a lot of superstars in this game but I don't think they're all like that. I don't think they're all willing to do whatever it takes for their team. That's what makes us special. That's what makes this team special. We have a lot of superstars, but they're willing to do whatever it takes to help us win the World Series. You saw that tonight.

"I've done some short rest stuff (in the playoffs). I've pitched on one day rest. I've never done no day's rest. ... (Yamamoto) is amazing. He really is." ■

Yoshinobu Yamamoto had just enough strength left in his arms to hoist the well-deserved World Series MVP trophy. (AP Images)

THE 2025 SEASON

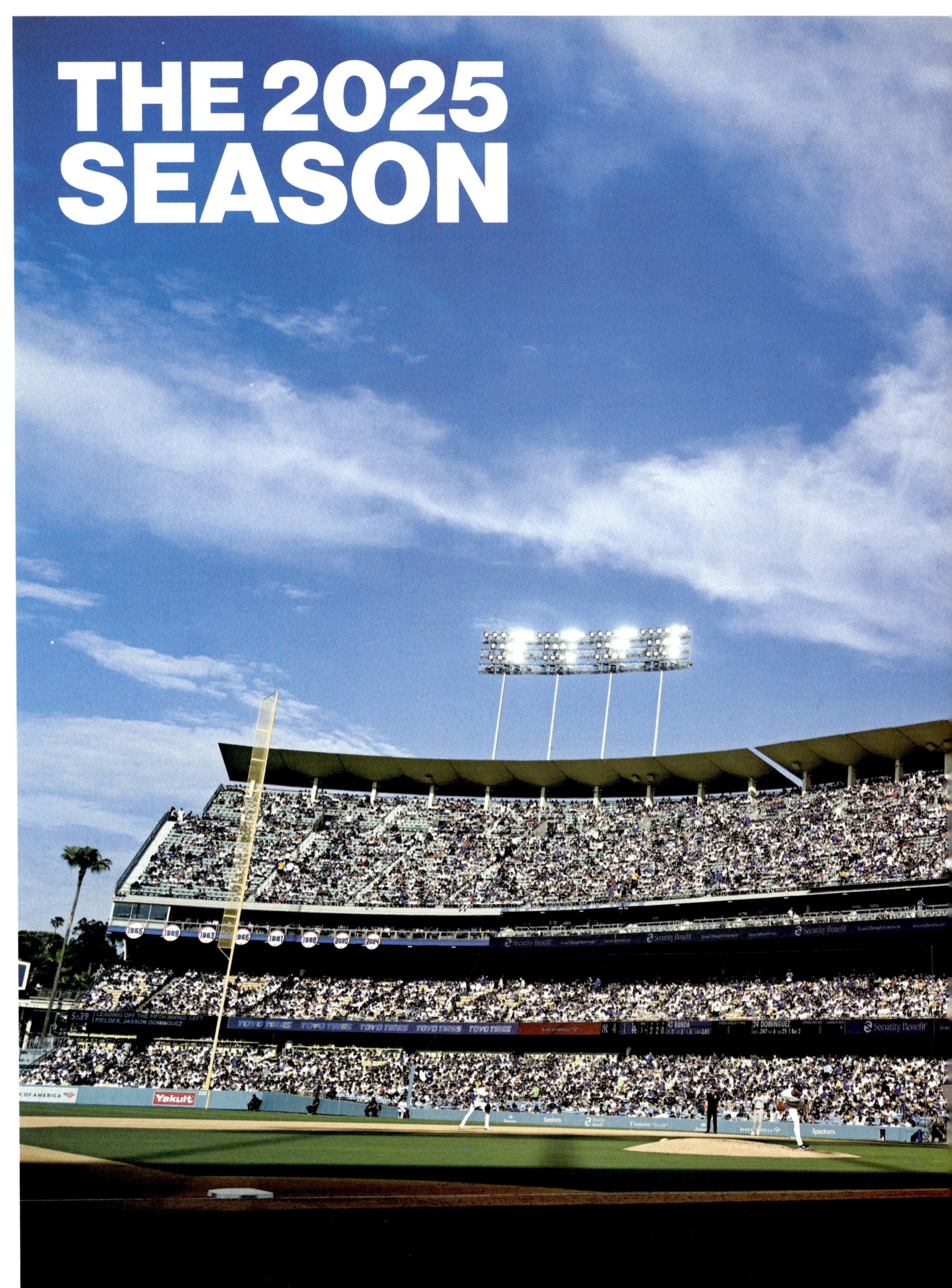

Los Angeles Daily News: Keith Birmingham

Nothing Left to Say

For Dodgers' Dave Roberts, 2 Rings, 4 More Years ... and Maybe Some Grace?

By Jim Alexander | March 11, 2025

The haters, if any remain, should stand down now.

All of those folks who have lambasted Dave Roberts over the years because his relief pitchers failed him, or because he wasn't as ebullient as Tom Lasorda, or for whatever reason – including some that might have been either incomprehensible or downright offensive? Surely you've seen the error of your ways by now, right?

He's entering his 10th season as Dodgers manager. He has managed teams to four World Series and won two in the last five seasons – and I'm trying hard not to make one more reference to 2017 and trash cans – and none of his teams have missed the postseason.

He's maybe the ideal manager for this era of baseball, – respectful of the game's analytics trend, yet uniquely skilled in dealing with and getting the most out of the men who populate his clubhouse, as the face of an organization that demands versatility and emphasizes positional flexibility. (Remember, as I've said before, there's a good reason why the job title is "manager.")

For example, there were the words with which he addressed his players early last spring at Camelback Ranch, when he talked about delivering in the biggest of moments in the postseason and, ideally, the World Series.

"I believe his exact words are, 'You need to want to be the guy,'" Max Muncy said before Game 3 in Yankee Stadium last October. "That's why we're all here. We all want to be in this situation. We all want to be the guy in that moment. ... That's definitely something that sticks out to you when your manager calls you out like that in spring training saying, 'Hey, you guys all need to want to be the guy in that situation. You can't leave it up to someone else.'"

Roberts has shown the same consistency, in demeanor and decisiveness, that he has asked of his players.

And now he's going to get paid.

The four-year extension that Roberts and the Dodgers have agreed to will not only double his pay but assure him of a record average annual value, slightly more than the $8 million per year Craig Counsell is getting from the deal he signed last year with the Chicago Cubs.

If I were Roberts, I'd call Counsell and start the conversation with, "Eight-point-one million a year," just to get a reaction. (Counsell would probably laugh.)

Let's see: Two rings, matching Lasorda (but in only nine years compared to Tommy's 19 full seasons), a record-setting contract, fairly unanimous respect among baseball people, total and unquestioned respect from those who play for him, and now maybe even some grudging respect from those among the fan base who have been ready to turn on him at the first sign of difficulty.

And another reminder: Roberts' regular-season winning percentage as a manager is .627, and his 851-507 includes an 0-1 record as interim manager of the Padres in 2015. (And don't think there aren't people in San Diego who still wonder if Padres front office boss A.J. Preller should have kept the guy who was already on staff when he, too, made a managerial change that fall.)

As we have noted before, Roberts' winning

Dave Roberts entered his 10th season as Dodgers manager with four World Series appearances under his belt, earning him a four-year extension. (Los Angeles Daily News: David Crane)

LA
Dodgers
30

SNELL
7
BETTS
50
LA

percentage is the best ever among those who have managed in the National or American leagues. The only ones better are Negro Leagues managers Bullet Rogan, Vic Harris, Rube Foster and Dave Malarcher, and Rogan and Foster have plaques in Cooperstown. By way of comparison, Walter Alston's winning percentage in 23 Dodgers' seasons was .558 (and he won four World Series). Lasorda's in 21 seasons was .526. Both are in the Hall of Fame, and it's certainly conceivable that Roberts, who turns 53 in May, will be enshrined at some point in the distant future.

And after Roberts' master class in marshaling his pitching resources and papering over an injury-ravaged staff in last October's run to a title, can we stop with the knee-jerk reactions to every decision?

An increasingly fatalistic fan base howled, for example, during a Labor Day weekend game in Phoenix last year when a game against the Diamondbacks got out of hand early, with Arizona taking an 8-0 lead in the second inning. Rather than dip into a bullpen that had been taxed already that weekend – eight pitchers on Friday, the night Clayton Kershaw left with a foot injury, and four more on Saturday, both in Dodgers victories – Roberts stayed with Justin Wrobleski into the sixth.

The fan reaction on social media was outrage and frenzy – *"He's not trying to win!!!"* – but consider: The Dodgers did lose that game, but it was the only blemish in a 6-1 stretch. Roberts was managing for the long haul, recognizing that sometimes it's best to save your best pitchers for when you really need them. If the benefits of that strategy weren't immediately obvious, they became so during the postseason when a Dodgers pitching staff that by October was running on fumes had enough to make it to the end.

Take Game 4 of the World Series in Yankee Stadium. A bullpen game turned ugly, the Dodgers were trailing 5-2 after three innings, and Roberts elected to stay away from his leverage relievers that night, using Landon Knack for four innings and Brent Honeywell for one with an eye toward what turned out to be the decisive Game 5. The Dodgers got to within a run in the top of the fifth, but the Yankees broke it open with six in the eighth in an 11-4 win.

Afterward Roberts said: "To have six guys in your 'pen that are feeling good, rested, I feel good about that."

The proof came the following evening, which is why the Dodgers will be receiving World Series rings at their second home game of 2025, March 28 against Detroit.

When Roberts receives his, the cheers had better be deafening. ■

Dave Roberts visits starting pitcher Blake Snell on the mound during a September game against the Philadelphia Phillies. (Los Angeles Daily News: Keith Birmingham)

STARTING PITCHER

18

YOSHINOBU YAMAMOTO

Dodgers Expect 'Good Things' from Yoshinobu Yamamoto in Year 2

By Bill Plunkett | March 26, 2025

From his first bullpen session this spring, there seemed to be something different about Yoshinobu Yamamoto.

"I think he's just comfortable," Dodgers pitching coach Mark Prior said this spring, putting his finger squarely on it. "It's a similar situation that we all go through – new environment, language barrier at times. I think 12 months, having the experience of last year – winning a World Series doesn't hurt.

"But he's just comfortable and confident. ... That's really the difference whereas last year there was some uncertainty – as there should be. Trying to figure out which is Field 1 and 2 (at Camelback Ranch). Just simple things like that. Even for our minor-leaguers and young guys, just having that 'been-there, done-that' type of thing puts those apprehensions at ease. Then he can just let his talent do what he does. That's been the thing. He's comfortable and confident. He knows he belongs. He pitched at an extremely high level on the big stages last year."

Yamamoto certainly looked comfortable at the Tokyo Dome last week. He held the Chicago Cubs to one run on three hits over five innings, winning the season-opening game. He will take the mound again Friday night at Dodger Stadium.

His Tokyo performance was a far cry from last year's worrisome MLB debut in South Korea.

Signed to the biggest contract ever given to a pitcher (who doesn't also DH) despite never having thrown a pitch in the major leagues, Yamamoto made his major-league debut in the Dodgers' second game against the San Diego Padres in Seoul. To say it didn't go well would be putting it mildly.

Yamamoto's first pitch as a major-leaguer was ripped for a 105.4-mph single by Xander Bogaerts. And things went downhill from there. Yamamoto lasted just one inning, allowing five runs on four hits and a walk. He hit a batter, threw a wild pitch and needed 43 water-torture pitches just to get three outs.

A career launch like that – with the anchor of a 12-year, $325 million contract weighted around his neck – could have crushed the confidence of a young pitcher, even one with the track record of success Yamamoto brought from Japan.

It did not. Over his next 13 starts, Yamamoto was 6-1 with a 2.34 ERA, holding major-league hitters to a .212 average and .593 OPS before missing three months with an injured shoulder.

"I think it speaks to his character in the sense that after that debacle, that rough start, to bounce back

Yoshinobu Yamamoto entered his second season in Los Angeles with a newfound confidence and ease that anchored the Dodgers' starting rotation. (Los Angeles Daily News: David Crane)

Dodger
18

like he did, it speaks to his compete and his character," Dodgers manager Dave Roberts said.

Yamamoto repeated the pattern in the postseason. He gave up five runs in three innings to the Padres in his postseason debut, losing Game 1 of the National League Division Series – but he gave up just three runs in 15⅔ innings over his next three postseason starts including Game 2 of the World Series when he held the New York Yankees to one hit into the seventh inning.

"Really watching him navigate the first playoff game – he gave up those runs but came back and battled and really took off after that," Dodgers general manager Brandon Gomes said. "I think there's a real confidence that, 'Hey, I can be one of the best pitchers in the game.' There's just been a different level of focus (this spring). Obviously, he's not dealing with as many adjustments this year. But his lives, his 'pens (live batting practice and bullpen sessions), there's a whole 'nother level of focus. I really think he's primed for a big year."

Roberts made the same prediction repeatedly this spring.

"Honestly, I'm expecting a lot of good things from Yoshinobu this year," Roberts said. "He got his feet wet last year and did a fantastic job for us. But he's ahead of where he was last year and that's exciting.

"There's a lot less unknown. I think where he's at physically and with his mechanics he's just ahead of where he was last year."

Roberts took it even farther after Yamamoto's start in Japan.

"I think that last year to this year, the confidence, the conviction that he has in throwing the fastball in the strike zone is much, much more convicted." Roberts said. "And so you saw that tonight. And so if he can do that – obviously (with) health – I see no reason why he won't be in the Cy Young conversation this season."

Yamamoto resists making too many comparisons between where he was a year ago at this time and how he feels in Year 2 in the big leagues. His "mental status is not much different," he said through his interpreter on the eve of the Tokyo Series, though he acknowledged learning "from that mistake, failure" in Korea.

"In terms of the preparation, there's not much difference," he said. "Last year, things didn't go my way. But this year I think I'm pretty happy with where I am." ■

Dodgers general manager Brandon Gomes praised Yoshinobu Yamamoto's new level of focus early on, accurately predicting an impactful sophomore season. (Los Angeles Daily News: David Crane)

Hollywood Beginning

Dodgers' Home Opener Gives Fans Another Chance to Celebrate 2024

By Jim Alexander | March 28, 2025

When you have something to celebrate – I mean, *really* celebrate – and you're located just down Sunset Blvd. from Hollywood, you use the resources available to you, right?

So instead of some generic concept such as defending a championship or running it back, it looks like the Dodgers' 2025 season will be known as "The Sequel." Though maybe the ballclub should re-think that, considering the number of sequels this town produces that aren't nearly as good as the originals.

But this one is off to a good start. After getting a jump on the rest of baseball with two victories over the Chicago Cubs in Tokyo last week, the Dodgers won their domestic Opening Day on Thursday, grabbing leads on home runs by Tommy Edman and Teoscar Hernández, getting an insurance run on Shohei Ohtani's second homer of the year, and holding on to beat Detroit, 5-4, and stay undefeated at 3-0.

Yes, the pre-game celebration Thursday began with a cinematic trailer, basically composed of the highlights from the original, the Dodgers' run to the 2024 championship. And the celebration of '24 and introduction of the '25 Dodgers that followed hit most of the high points, including an appearance by Ice Cube, driving a classic Chevy convertible (license plate: THEBLUEZ) with the Commissioner's Trophy riding shotgun.

Obviously, Mr. Cube is now a full member of the Dodger family, given that he also came back for the traditional "It's Time For Dodger Baseball" refrain as first pitch approached. No word on whether Fat Joe, the Bronx rapper who was meant to provide the rebuttal at last year's World Series Game 3 in Yankee Stadium, made an appearance at the Yankees' home opener Thursday. Given the scathing reviews of his October performance, I suspect not.

The Dodger players were introduced coming out from behind a curtain in center field, with players trotting from dead center to join their teammates along the third base line. I'm not sure the blue carpet works as well on Opening Day in The Ravine as the red carpet does on, say, Oscars night.

But there was the trophy, and the hoisting of the 2024 championship banner on one of the center field flagpoles, conducted by members of the Guggenheim ownership group including controlling owner Mark Walter, Todd Boehly, Magic Johnson, Billie Jean King and her partner, Ilana Kloss. (Hall of Famers Magic and Billie Jean seemed to be doing most of the heavy work). There was the unveiling of the 2024 championship icon down the right field line by Pasadena Fire Department captain Jodi Sicker and Los Angeles fire captain Jerry Puga, an appropriate nod to what L.A. has had to deal with in the first three months of this year.

And while I hate to bring this up, those eight championship icons have a pattern: Two from the 1950s ('55 in Brooklyn, '59 in L.A.), two from the '60s ('63 and '65), two from the '80s ('81 and '88) and now two from this decade (2020 and '24). That historic pattern doesn't bode well for a repeat in '25, but who's superstitious?

Rapper Ice Cube brings out the 2024 World Series Trophy prior to the Dodgers' home opener against the Tigers. (Los Angeles Daily News: Keith Birmingham)

LA
LA

But even running that flag up the pole wasn't the *piece de resistance*. TV play-by-play guy Joe Davis brought out Freddie Freeman and his family, had a brief chat with Freddie's dad, Fred Freeman, and then referenced his call for Fox last fall of Freeman's walk-off grand slam in Game 1 – "Gibby, meet Freddie" – by beckoning ... guess who, to greet Freeman and throw out the first ball?

Right. And it will say here that Kirk Gibson, whose original World Series Game 1 walk-off homer in 1988 also led to a World Series championship, threw a perfect strike to Freeman. Yeah, in reality it was a little low, but why spoil a good story?

Baseball, in many ways, is all about the story – the history, and the indelible moments we witness firsthand and still have in our mind's eye three decades or so later. Ceremonies like these resonate in a ballpark far more than they would in any other sports venue.

So consider this a double celebration. Friday night the Dodgers get their championship rings. Manager Dave Roberts said he hadn't seen them yet, but expect gaudy. And a multi-day celebration is certainly in character for an organization that, decades ago, decided a one-day helmet giveaway wasn't enough and turned it into Helmet Weekend. (Sold out the weekend, too, as I recall.)

"I think it gives the fans an opportunity to have something unique and special for two days in a row," Roberts said. "And the fans that aren't here today, that can come tomorrow, get something unique as well."

Given that those fans haven't had a chance to have their own mass celebration since last November's parade, back-to-back ceremonies actually make sense.

Then again, baseball is also about the here and now.

Blake Snell was OK in his five innings of work Thursday, getting out of a first and third jam in the second, loading the bases and wild-pitching a run home in the fourth and giving up two hits, a walk and a scoring fly ball in the fifth before calling it a day. He still got the win, thanks to Hernández's three-run homer off reigning AL Cy Young Award winner Tarik Skubal in the bottom of the fifth.

And while Tanner Scott appeared to be signed with the closer role in mind, Roberts isn't afraid to shuffle things at the back end. Scott pitched the eighth and gave up a triple to former Dodger Zach McKinstry and a scoring fly ball to make it 5-4. Blake Treinen pitched the ninth, put the tying and go-ahead runs on base and wiggled out of the jam.

Teoscar was the only Hernández on the premises, since Kiké Hernandez was home sick with what appeared to be some of the same symptoms that had laid Mookie Betts low. Teoscar also hit in the No. 3 spot in the lineup ahead of Freeman, and that could be an interesting wrinkle. Roberts talked before the game of a "Teoscar tax" for any pitcher having to wade through that lineup and face Freeman for a third time, and it was Hernández's third at-bat when he picked on Skubal's first pitch for that three-run homer.

"In that situation, because I know I have Freddie behind me, they're not going to pitch around me too much," he said.

That would be taxing for any pitcher. ■

Mookie Betts celebrates Tommy Edman's second-inning solo home run during the Dodgers' 2025 home opener. (Los Angeles Daily News: Keith Birmingham)

blue
CALIFORNIA
Dodgers
50

FIRST BASEMAN

5

FREDDIE FREEMAN

Dodgers' Freddie Freeman Sees 3,000 Career Hits as 'Not Unrealistic'

By Bill Plunkett | May 12, 2025

No sport loves its numbers more than baseball. Freddie Freeman shares that reverence, recognizing their utility in the ultimate goal – winning.

"Numbers are still a huge thing," he said over the weekend while in the process of putting up a stat line that earned him National League Player of the Week honors. "Everybody looks at numbers. Everyone loves round numbers.

"As you're a kid growing up, for me it was 500 home runs, 3,000 hits. Those were the numbers. … Round numbers are really cool."

Three thousand hits is a round number only 33 players in the history of Major League Baseball have reached (most recently, Miguel Cabrera in April 2022). It represents "longevity, consistency" to Freeman, two traits that characterize his career, now in its 16th season. And it is a number Freeman would like to reach.

With a four-hit game on Sunday, Freeman has 2,308 career hits, the most among active players. Houston's Jose Altuve is next at 2,270.

"It would mean a lot," he said. "I've always valued hits. I know hits and average have dwindled in value in analytics and all that. But I value it. If I hit .300 and I play every day that means, with the way I walk as well, I'm on base close to the upper 200s. That creates traffic. That creates stress and different things. So I value it.

"Obviously I'm 35 now. I'll be 36 at the end of the year. So I've got less than a handful of years left. You do think about those type of things. But that's not the forefront obviously. Winning is at the forefront for me. But if I'm on the field and I'm healthy, I believe in myself that potentially I have a good chance of making it."

Dodgers manager Dave Roberts thinks Freeman has more than just a good chance.

"He'll get there. He will absolutely get there. There's no doubt in my mind," Roberts said.

"I think it represents consistency and longevity and that's something that he really hangs his hat on. Nowadays, people talk about slug and there's certainly value to it. But to accrue a number like that – consistency, longevity, availability, reliability, all of those things for your teammate and your manager, that's invaluable."

Freeman – a career .301 hitter who has averaged 181 hits for every 162 games in his career – has done the numbers on what it will take to get to 3,000.

"Obviously it's not set in stone. I have two years left on this contract (after 2025)," he said. "Then I would like to play two more years. I would turn 40 in September of 2029. So including this year, if I were to do 150 hits for all five years – just an average – you reach it. Obviously … Father Time, you never know

Freddie Freeman poses for a photo with Kirk Gibson, after the latter threw out the first pitch for the team's home opener. The two players are forever linked by their World Series Game 1 walk-off home runs in 2024 and 1988, respectively. (Los Angeles Daily News: Keith Birmingham)

LA
Dodgers
5
23
FERNANDO
34
CHAMPIONS

when that's going to hit. I'm trying to keep it away as long as I can. If I can have decent years this year and the next couple years, it's an easier reach."

The challenges become greater as you age. Freeman certainly has found that out over the past year. He missed 15 games last season due to a broken finger, a severely sprained ankle and his son's illness. It was the most action he had missed since 2017, when he was hit by a pitch and suffered a broken wrist.

The ankle injury has lingered into this season even after surgery last fall. Freeman admits he is playing at less than 100%. The 2024 World Series MVP gets 90 minutes of treatment on his ankle before every game and more after the game. He plays with it taped and with heel lifts in his cleats to lessen the impact of running and has grudgingly agreed there might be value in taking an occasional day off.

With all that, he is batting .376 with a 1.170 OPS.

"I'm obviously not feeling 100%. But I am feeling good enough out there where I'm not thinking about it," he said Sunday. "But I do have a lot that goes into each and every day to get on the field. Ultimately I feel good enough.

"Thomas (Albert, Dodgers head athletic trainer) thinks in a couple months, maybe after the All-Star break, I might not have to do as much treatment. I'm looking forward to that."

In some scenarios, Freeman would be entering the DH phase of his career. Shohei Ohtani's presence eliminates that option with the Dodgers – and Freeman rejects it anyway. It is not the way he wants to reach whatever milestones he reaches in the twilight years of his career.

"I don't want to," he said. "There's also another number that I really like that people might not think is special but it's special to me. That's games played at first base. Eddie Murray has that (2,413 – Freeman is at 2,035).

"That would mean something because it's hard to play every day – at any position – and that's a lot of games played. That means you were good enough for an organization to put you out there for that many games. That means something to me. That means you were consistently good every year and they valued having you out there on the field every day."

Freeman is hopeful the Dodgers still value him enough in two years to offer him another contract – the opportunity to market a march to 3,000 would certainly have value for the Dodgers as well – and rejects the narrative of returning to Atlanta at that point to finish his career where it began.

He also rejects the idea that he could be the last player to join the 3,000-hit club, a notion raised in some quarters because of the lower offensive numbers in the current era and the de-emphasis on batting average.

Beyond Freeman and Altuve (who just turned 35), only two other active players have more than 2,000 hits and both (Pittsburgh outfielder Andrew McCutchen and New York Yankees first baseman Paul Goldschmidt) are older than Freeman.

Some young player out there has started his own march to 3,000, Freeman said, and he ticks off the requirements.

"The younger guys still have a chance," he said, citing Kansas City Royals shortstop Bobby Witt Jr. as a prime example. "You've got to get to the big leagues early. You've got to be consistent. You've got to be good enough that they want you to play every day – which is hard to do in this game. Be able to hit right- and left(-handed pitching). To be in the lineup a lot."

Freeman has done all of those things throughout his career and now sees "a light at the end of the tunnel" that makes reaching 3,000 hits "not unrealistic now."

"I honestly respect him saying he's chasing 3,000," Roberts said. "I don't see anything wrong with chasing consistency. I think that's great. You're essentially saying, 'Yeah, I'm chasing being really good for four more years.' What's wrong with that? There's nothing wrong with that." ■

Despite a lingering ankle injury that carried over from 2024, Freddie Freeman has continued to put up productive batting numbers while playing first base. (Los Angeles Daily News: Keith Birmingham)

YAAMAVA
RESORT & CASIN
AT SAN MANUEL

Elite Company

Clayton Kershaw Joins Distinguished List with 3,000th Strikeout

By Jim Alexander | July 3, 2025

If we needed one more reminder that striking out major league hitters isn't easy – much less striking out 3,000 in a career – we got it Wednesday night.

Yes, Clayton Kershaw made history against the Chicago White Sox, becoming the 20th pitcher in MLB history to reach 3,000, just the fourth left-hander and only the third to strike 'em all out while playing his whole career for one team.

He needed three strikeouts going into the game, and it took him six innings and an even 100 pitches to get the third one, getting Vinny Capra on a slider for a called third strike to end the inning – three pitches after Max Muncy hurt his left knee in a collision with Michael A. Taylor while tagging him out trying to steal third.

This night was an appropriate demonstration of the pitcher Kershaw has become in his 18th season as a Dodger. The fastball no longer sizzles – Wednesday night he averaged 89.4 with his four-seam fastball, half an mph better than his season average – but he still got 15 swings and misses, nine of them on a slider that averaged 85.4 mph.

That slider, incidentally, he characterized as "so bad." The pitch to Capra "wasn't a good one," he said. "Wasn't where it was supposed to be. I'm just glad I got him out."

The fact that Kershaw didn't have full command of his out pitch but persevered and got it done anyway should be one tipoff as to why Dodger fans treasure him so, and why Wednesday night they seemed to want the accomplishment for him as much as or more than he wanted it for himself.

And it also said as much about the 18-year relationship between Kershaw and the Dodgers, and Kershaw and their fans, as it did about the number 3,000.

It was a relationship that began May 25, 2008, with a strikeout of Skip Schumaker – the very first hitter he faced – in a six-inning no-decision against the St. Louis Cardinals in his major league debut. Kershaw struck out seven that day, which suggested that the spring training game televised back to L.A. a couple of months before wasn't a mirage, and that when Vin Scully gushed about the young pitcher after a 12-to-6 curveball froze Boston's Sean Casey for a called third strike, this actually was a precursor to the real thing.

Fast forward to Wednesday night. Kershaw, not usually concerned with personal milestones, really did want No. 3,000 badly this night, to reward the home fans (and to avoid having to prolong the suspense until his next start next week in Milwaukee). The fans might have wanted it more. They roared when Kershaw got to two strikes. They groaned when those at-bats ended in something other than a strikeout. And they rooted him home, through his six innings and 100 pitches.

"I think the fans' reaction more than anything was so special to me," he said. "Before the game, kind of feeling the energy in the crowd. And it was definitely palpable. I think that's the right word. I think you can feel it. And then like, after the fifth inning and going back out for the sixth and that crowd ovation was something that I'll never forget for sure."

This was, as Dodgers manager Dave Roberts put it before the game, one last box to check on Kershaw's list of career accomplishments. Kershaw has won three Cy Young Awards and an MVP, led the majors in ERA four times and the National League a fifth, led the NL in strikeouts three times – and all of baseball in 2015 (with 301) – and has thrown a no-hitter.

And with two World Series championship rings he

Clayton Kershaw tips his cap to the Dodger Stadium crowd after striking out Vinny Capra of the Chicago White Sox for his 3,000th career strikeout. (Los Angeles Daily News: Keith Birmingham)

has erased the stigma of previous postseason failures, though in fairness too many starts on short rest played a role in those postseason stumbles early in his career. (So, too, did Game 5 of the 2017 World Series in Houston when, as we now are well aware, the Astros knew exactly what was coming and kept laying off of Kershaw's slider.)

Now Kershaw joins a distinguished group in the 3,000-strikeout club. But in another sense, he stands alone.

He's the 20th to reach that figure. Only three others are left-handers: Randy Johnson, Steve Carlton and CC Sabathia. Only two others spent their entire careers with one team: Walter Johnson with the Washington Senators from 1907 to '27, and Bob Gibson with the St. Louis Cardinals from 1959 to '75.

Only Kershaw has done both.

Of those he now joins in the 3,000 Club, Kershaw said the career that most resonated with him was that of fellow lefty Sabathia, who will be inducted into the Hall of Fame this month. But it's for a reason you might not expect if you weren't watching closely.

"I remember watching CC when he got traded over to the Brewers (by Cleveland in 2008), and he pitched on three days' rest constantly to try to get them in the playoffs all the way through, all the way through, all the way through, and just really put his team on his back," Kershaw said. "And it really just kind of resonated with me, like what a starting pitcher can be and what he can do for a team like that, and just kind of no regard for himself, doing everything he can to get his team into the playoffs. And he succeeded, he did it. So just to see him get that 3,000, I just have a lot of respect for him. I think that was pretty awesome."

If you think that sounds like the sort of stuff Kershaw attempted to do when his own team reached the postseason in later years, maybe that's where it came from.

And there is another aspect to this, in those circle-of-life moments you might notice if you watch Dodgers telecasts. You see it frequently: Kershaw, on days when he's not pitching, perched on the dugout railing, watching, talking to his fellow pitchers and almost certainly imparting the wisdom of one who has seen and done so much.

"A lot, a lot," Roberts said when I asked him if Kershaw's influence rubbed off on the youngsters on the staff. "You know guys grab him (and talk), but for the most part, I think that (it's) just kind of how he goes about it. He's always talking the game. He's watching the game, more importantly. He's very consistent. Even yesterday I was watching in the 'pen. He was doing his dry work (going through his pitching motion without a ball). And this is something he's done for 18 years, the day before a start.

"Those things are things that players see, young pitchers see: The value of strike one, the value of going deeper in games and you know, commanding your secondaries (pitches) and things like that. So that's something that you know guys not only that are here with us now, but that have been with him in years past that are taking to some of the stuff that he's taught them."

And I'd imagine Kershaw has dropped the following nugget into those conversations more than once.

"I told my teammates (after Wednesday's game), individual awards are great, but if you don't have anybody to celebrate with, it doesn't matter," he said. "And so to have that room full of guys – coaches, strength staff, training staff, front office, everybody – just really be happy for me is just awesome. They were in it with me, and it was an amazing night." ■

After reaching a milestone 3,000 strikeouts, Clayton Kershaw was presented with the Dodger Stadium pitching rubber. (Los Angeles Daily News: Keith Birmingham)

Dodgers
KERSHAW
22

Celebrating the Journey

Dodgers Toasting Small Moments Has Become Big Part of Team Culture

By Bill Plunkett | July 10, 2025

The ritual after big victories is long-standing and familiar. It calls for beer and champagne.

But the Dodgers have created a tradition of their own for the small victories that come along the way – and it calls for tequila.

For two years now, each time the Dodgers have won a series – something they had done for seven consecutive series before their current six-game losing streak put the tequila on ice – the players gather in the clubhouse, infielder Miguel Rojas recaps the highlights of the series, picks a series MVP and the players down shots of tequila (apple juice for any non-drinkers).

The ritual ends with Rojas handing his phone to the series MVP, who takes a selfie with all of his teammates behind him. Rojas collects the photos and shares them in a players-only group chat.

"At the end of the day, it's baseball and it's our job. But it's just a game," pitcher Dustin May said of the tradition. "Being able to take the little positives and have a little team talk after, put some of the exciting moments of the series on blast – it's cool."

The Dodgers are the eighth team that relief pitcher Anthony Banda has played for during a peripatetic major-league career that has allowed him to sample an assortment of team cultures.

"I was expecting something because any time a team wins a series there's some kind of celebration," the reliever said of joining the Dodgers early last season. "The drinking aspect of it was new because I don't think I'd been on a team that did shots. It was more of a quick 'Hoorah' and then move on.

"What I like most about it is how Miggy Ro or whoever is leading the celebration will point out what was good, the highlights of the series. It seems like he's very on point with a lot of it, because he never misses any type of deal. Like, he'll talk about things like what Ben (Casparius) and Jack (Dreyer) did pitching out of the bullpen."

The tradition's origin story dates to May 2023 after the Dodgers swept the San Diego Padres in a three-game series at Dodger Stadium. They had taken two out of three in San Diego a week earlier, doubling their dose of revenge for the previous fall's loss to the Padres in the playoffs.

Rojas and outfielders Jason Heyward and David Peralta were all new to the team that year and took note of how business-like the Dodgers were in the aftermath of a significant regular-season moment.

"We started talking. 'These guys aren't really celebrating,'" Rojas said. "We all felt like this team was all about business at the time and celebrating wins in the regular season would be too much for them.

"I feel like getting used to winning in the regular season was a thing for them."

The three took their idea to the team's established veterans – "the big guys – Mookie (Betts), Freddie (Freeman), Kersh (Clayton Kershaw), Will (Smith) and Barnesy (Austin Barnes), guys that had been here for a long time" – and pitched them on making "a little bit of a culture change."

Dustin May reacts after inducing an inning-ending double play against the Atlanta Braves. (Los Angeles Daily News: Keith Birmingham)

LA
Dodgers
85

RUSHING
68
Dodgers
16

The tradition took hold and now includes other individual achievements that might otherwise get overlooked. The team toasts players who reach 10 years' service time (a significant MLB benchmark that brings pension and other benefits), rookies who record their first win or hit and veterans who reach milestones – for example, Clayton Kershaw's 3,000th strikeout and Teoscar Hernandez's 1,000th career hit recently.

"It's just a really cool way to recognize the good things that are happening during the course of the season," Freddie Freeman said. "The ebbs and flows of the season – you'll go through some rough times and then all of a sudden you win eight series in a row and you're doing a lot of tequila shots.

"It's more in our group. It's not about anyone else. It's just showing appreciation for one another."

Both Rojas and Heyward are tequila drinkers and settled on a Clase Azul reposado tequila that comes in a hand-painted, decorative bottle. Third baseman Max Muncy foots the bill for the liquor (which can cost as much as $150 a bottle) and someone from the clubhouse staff is responsible for making sure the supply is always on hand. They upgraded the tequila for each playoff series victory on the way to the World Series title last year.

"The bottle kind of looks like a microphone because it's got the little cup," Rojas said. "So I talk about what happened during that series – maybe a guy hit a homer or moved a guy over. It doesn't have to be big things. It could be the bullpen guys or whatever. Then we always take a selfie afterwards that we put in our group chat and we save it.

"Last year when we won the World Series, I put the pictures together and I sent them to the guys – a lot of guys in that picture are without clothes on so it's private. But maybe 50 years from now you're going to look at your phone and you're going to have all these pictures from an amazing 2024. We're probably going to have a couple Hall of Famers here, so we're going to have a couple pictures with them. I think it's a pretty good thing to have."

Banda said he finds himself flipping through the photos at night sometimes, smiling at the different faces. One of those future Hall of Famers, Freeman, acknowledged that the expectations that come with playing for the Dodgers can lead to taking things for granted at times.

"You can get into that habit. When I came over, that's the way it was," he said. "That's the beauty of this game. New guys come in and you talk about it and you see how things are going and it's 'Oh, I've got this idea. Why don't we try this?' and the next thing you know everyone loves it.

"Every day we get up and we're trying to get ready for that game and trying to win that game and you go to bed and you get up and do it again over and over. When you throw in a little wrinkle – hey, wait, we just won a series and this guy did this and that guy did that. I think it's been really cool." ■

Will Smith is greeted by teammates at home plate after hitting a walk-off home run to defeat the San Diego Padres. (Los Angeles Daily News: David Crane)

A League of His Own

Shohei Ohtani is Easing Back into Pitching While Amazing His Teammates with His Ability to Juggle Both Roles

By Bill Plunkett | July 14, 2025

They saw it coming.

For more than a year, Shohei Ohtani's return to the mound, to two-way player status, was a topic of near-constant conversation and speculation. But it's still impressive to see it up close.

"He's almost the best hitter in the game and he's almost the best pitcher in the game. It's just amazing," Dodgers first baseman Freddie Freeman, one of his teammates in Tuesday's All-Star Game, said of watching Ohtani in full this season.

"It's like he's in his own league. We all did that in Little League, but he's doing it in the big leagues. It's special."

The Dodgers have eased Ohtani back into two-way play. He pitched a third inning for the first time in his fifth and most recent start on Saturday in San Francisco. The 36 pitches he threw that afternoon are the most they have asked him to throw in any of his weekly starts.

"Obviously early on we were planning him not to pitch with us until more of a higher buildup, as far as four or five innings," Dodgers manager Dave Roberts said. "But his anxiousness to get back on a big-league mound kind of prompted that. And then from that point on, it's been pretty deliberate. That's how it played out.

"I think it's also been helpful for Shohei to kind of dip his toe in the water, as far as logging some innings going into the (All-Star) break, having somewhat of a foundation going out through the second half."

Ohtani might have forced the issue, essentially convincing the Dodgers he could continue his rehab on the mound in major-league games rather than facing minor-league hitters in simulated games. But he was in agreement with the slow pace of his return to pitching.

"In a rehab progression, it's really important to just take one step at a time," Ohtani said through his interpreter recently. "There are times when I may be able to go another inning, but it's really important not to take unnecessary risks and make sure that I can progress consistently. It's always been this way in terms of my rehab progression. So I'm following what the team is also asking me as well."

Nonetheless, he announced his return to pitching with authority, throwing a 101.7 mph fastball in the first inning of his third start. It was the fastest pitch of his MLB career. Possibly aided by knowing his outings are going to be short, Ohtani's 63 four-seam fastballs have averaged a career-high 98.2 mph.

But it has been more than that. So far, batters have hit .111 off his sweeper and .167 off his slider. According to Statcast bat tracking, none of his 140 pitches so far this season have been hit on the barrel of the bat.

"We all knew that he threw hard," Dodgers pitcher Clayton Kershaw said. "But he's got really good stuff. He's got multiple pitches. He's got six pitches, seven pitches – I don't even know how many he's got. His command – for not pitching for two years – is really

Dodgers teammates mob Shohei Ohtani after his walk-off home run against the Atlanta Braves in April. Ohtani continued his high production at the plate after returning to pitching duties following rehab from elbow surgery. (Los Angeles Daily News: Keith Birmingham)

OHTANI
17
Dodgers
86

good. He doesn't have too many misses.

"I guess we shouldn't be surprised because it's Shohei. But it's been impressive – really impressive."

Ohtani, who will bat leadoff for the National League but will not pitch in Tuesday's All-Star Game, gave up a run on two hits in his first inning against the San Diego Padres on June 16 – his first game action as a pitcher since August 2023. Since then, he has pitched eight scoreless innings, allowing just three singles, walking two and striking out 10.

"It's awesome," Dodgers relief pitcher Alex Vesia said. "I'm going to use that word because it is so cool for him to pitch and literally walk off the mound, get checked (for sticky stuff by an umpire), get his helmet on and – first up. To me that is so cool.

"It is crazy. I've been more and more surprised by the velocity and the command and stuff. We didn't know what it was going to be like. We had no idea. But if you talk to him, I bet he knew exactly what it was going to look like. That's confidence. That's preparation. That's there. And that's why he is who he is."

The three-time league MVP remains an elite hitter and tone-setter at the top of the lineup. He leads the NL with 32 home runs to go with 12 doubles, seven triples, 62 walks, 60 RBIs and 91 runs scored while slashing .276/.382/.605.

Now, he is again showing off his other impressive skill – juggling.

He spent last season balancing his preparations as a hitter with the requirements of his rehab from the September 2023 elbow surgery. He handled that well enough to put up baseball's first 50/50 season. This year, the need to balance his work as a hitter with his preparations to start on the mound once a week, game planning and studying scouting reports for each, has been a new challenge – but one familiar to Ohtani.

"He does it really, really well," Kershaw said. "Nothing seems to overwhelm him. He just kind of knows what he has to do and he does it. There's not many people that could do that. There's only one of them."

Vesia has observed the juggling act with interest.

"His schedule has changed a little bit where he has to incorporate the pitching side of things," he said. "It's different because it's not a normal throwing program like myself. It is different the way he has to plan out his day to not only play catch, focus on pitching but then focus on hitting and go about that. So it's been really interesting to watch him go about his business.

"It's sticking to his routine day in, day out and knowing that it works for him. This isn't something that just popped up yesterday. This is years, going back to when he was in Japan. This is a routine that he knows. Obviously if I were to jump in tomorrow and try that it would probably be pretty hard. To do that at this level – plus he's come back and each start he's gotten better and better."

On the mound, Ohtani takes on another task, calling most of his own pitches (as he did with the Angels).

"That's a hard thing to do too. I don't think I could do that," said Kershaw, a three-time Cy Young Award winner. "To have that kind of feel for what you want to do – it's just impressive. I don't know what else to say."

Vesia took it a step further. He said he would be surprised if Ohtani didn't want to call his own pitches "because he's the most prepared person I've ever met." Vesia thinks having the perspective of a hitter while pitching is an advantage for Ohtani, he said.

"I do," Vesia said. "I don't think like a hitter. I think like a pitcher. He's got both. That's definitely a very good insight for him. To see it from both lenses, that's cool."

And he seems to be enjoying it. Roberts said the Dodgers have learned this year that Ohtani has "more of an edge" to his personality when he's pitching.

"I think he loves pitching. I think he loves it – I think he loves it almost more than hitting," Freeman said. "The way you can control a game on the mound, it's all about you. I think he loves it. I grew up pitching and I loved it. That was so much fun.

"There's so much on you. I think he loves that. He's almost the best hitter in the game and he's almost the best pitcher in the game. It's just amazing." ■

Shohei Ohtani took the mound for the first time in a Dodgers uniform against the Padres at Dodger Stadium on June 16. (Los Angeles Daily News: David Crane)

Dodgers
17

DESIGNATED HITTER/STARTING PITCHER

17

SHOHEI OHTANI

Two-way Star Shohei Ohtani a True Phenomenon

By Jim Alexander | August 7, 2025

There are those throughout baseball, I am sure, who remain convinced that Shohei Ohtani would be better as either a hitter *or* a pitcher, and that trying to do both is ultimately a fool's errand.

I admit there are times that has crossed my mind as well, wondering how long he can maintain what, in essence, are two different jobs for a Dodgers organization whose mantra might as well be "Championship or bust."

But then there are games like Wednesday afternoon, which serve as reminders that we are seeing something none of us has ever witnessed. No matter how fervent a Dodgers fan you are, and how much the wins and losses matter – and they do – sometimes it's worth pausing to remind ourselves how special, how extraordinary this is.

Maybe it will impede the Dodgers' quest to repeat as World Series champs, or maybe it won't – and certainly, Shohei wasn't the one making mistakes in the late innings of Wednesday's 5-3 loss to the St. Louis Cardinals. But my goodness, isn't it worth it to just watch the show?

Wednesday against the Cardinals, Ohtani pitched four innings, struck out eight, and allowed a run on two third-inning hits that strung together wouldn't have left the infield: A pop-up by Jordan Walker that second baseman Miguel Rojas lost in the sun, and a gutsy two-out squeeze bunt by Brendan Donovan that scored Walker from third.

Then Ohtani wiped out that deficit in the bottom of the inning with a two-run, 440-foot blast into the pavilion in left center ... which, as fate would have it, was his 1,000th career hit in his eight major league seasons. Add his five seasons for the Nippon Ham Fighters in Japan's Pacific League and he now has 1,296 hits, 312 home runs and 788 RBIs.

Ohtani might not catch new Hall of Famer Ichiro Suzuki's 4,367 hits between MLB and Nippon Professional Baseball, but he's only 30. He's got time to chip away. And it's probably safe to say that they'll be readying a space for Ohtani's plaque in Cooperstown five years after this ride ends.

Ichiro did have one pitching appearance in his career, by the way, a lost-cause inning with Miami in 2015 when he was 41. Ichiro's career ERA: 9.00. Shohei's, after Wednesday: 2.36 in eight starts this season, 2.98 in this country's big leagues and 2.74 counting his five seasons in Japan.

Again: We are seeing something we've never seen

A singular talent in baseball's modern era, Shohei Ohtani continues to impress players and fans alike with his ability to juggle pitching and designated hitter roles into the prime of his career. (Los Angeles Daily News: David Crane)

LA
34
LA
dgers
17

before, a baseball player willing, determined and able to excel at two diametrically opposed skills. Last season, Ohtani's third league MVP campaign was a season for the ages offensively. You can argue – and I would – that this one, given the degree of difficulty, is even more amazing.

Pitching involves meetings to go over the opposing hitters on days when he starts, plus bullpens and side sessions in between starts. That's on top of his preparation as a hitter, going over those scouting reports.

And consider: Rather than taking it easy the day before a start, as other pitchers might, Ohtani was 2 for 4 with three runs scored on Tuesday night.

Let's break down Wednesday's performance further. He struck out Iván Herrera to end the third, his fifth K of the day and an inning in which he threw five of his six 100 mph pitches on the day (and also gave up that lone run). Then, as the third hitter in the bottom of the third, he hit Matthew Liberatore's 92 mph sinker halfway up the pavilion for his 39th homer of the year, with an exit velocity of 109.5, and a 2-1 lead.

And then he went out the next inning and struck out the side.

Afterward, he was asked if he did anything particular on days he pitches to make sure his offense didn't suffer.

"I don't really try to think too differently on days that I pitch and hit and on days that I only hit," he responded through interpreter Will Ireton.

Dodgers manager Dave Roberts said there has been something of a recalibration on Ohtani's part after nearly two full years, from August of 2023 to June of '25, in which he didn't pitch while recovering from his second elbow surgery.

"We talked about the meetings, the prep, the bullpen, going three innings, four innings, the postgame treatment with the arm," Roberts said before the game. "All that stuff matters. So yes, he's just kind of getting re-acclimated to doing that.

"... He's still sort of getting adjusted to this lifestyle as far as the day-to-day. I don't think he's there yet. I think it's only going to get better as he gets more time (at it)."

As for now, Ohtani will be a five-inning pitcher at most, and Roberts said some of that involves acknowledging the stress to the body of pitching. "Going forward, we'll see if that changes," he said. "But I think, for sure, for the next few turns, I don't see him getting beyond five."

And yes, there was a dropoff when he left Wednesday's game. Justin Wrobleski had plenty of baserunners in his three innings and gave up a run. Alex Vesia gave up the lead in a prolonged eighth inning that featured a key throwing error by rookie Alex Freeland, and trading deadline acquisition Brock Stewart gave up two hits, a walk and hit a batter as the Cardinals padded their lead in the ninth.

Keep in mind that Ohtani was pitching and hitting in Anaheim, too, and it was when he was an Angel that MLB adjusted the designated hitter rule to allow a pitcher – OK, to allow Ohtani – to stay in the game as DH after he'd been removed as a pitcher. Best decision the Lords of Baseball have made in a long time.

But this was pointed out to me, and it makes sense: With the impact Ohtani has had in L.A. and on the game as a whole in a little more than a season and a half – not only on the field but in popularity and economic impact – it might be hard to remember that he was a two-time MVP as an Angel.

And if you're an Angels fan, would you rather remember or forget?

After starting as pitcher for the Dodgers, Shohei Ohtani prepares to go to bat in the leadoff spot against the San Diego Padres. (Los Angeles Daily News: David Crane)

GUGGENHEIM

Snapping Out of It

Mookie Betts' Fresh Start Helps Dodgers Sweep Padres

By Jim Alexander | August 17, 2025

A week or so ago, Dodgers star Mookie Betts talked about reacting to a nearly season-long slump by giving up the chase for individual stats and going at-bat to at-bat, with an emphasis on whatever benefits the team the most.

It's working. And maybe it's contagious, and if so, perhaps the Dodgers have less to worry about than we anticipated just days before.

They were dreadfully down just a few days ago, a four-game losing streak punctuated by blown saves and runners left on base, capping a 12-21 stretch, which in turn dissipated what had been a nine-game division lead.

They are riding high again, just three games later, after Sunday's 5-4 victory over the San Diego Padres completed a three-game sweep and put the Dodgers back up by two games in the National League West.

And Betts, relieved of worrying about individual honors in large part because of what for him is a sickly slash line – .242 batting average, .312 on base percentage, .371 slugging percentage – put the crowning touch on Sunday's triumph with his 13th home run of the season leading off the eighth inning, on a 2-and-0 pitch by Padres relief stud Robert Suarez, to break a 4-4 tie.

To clarify, this is what Betts told reporters two Fridays ago, in the wake of an extended slump – possibly the residual effects of last season's broken hand, possibly influenced by the position switch that has made him a full-time shortstop – that kept him out of the All-Star Game and has resulted in career lows in several offensive categories:

"My season's kind of over. We're going to have to chalk that up as not a great season. But I can go out and help the boys win every night, do something, get an RBI, make a play, do something that I'm going to have to shift my focus there. Obviously, everyone wants to have great seasons, but it's a lot easier when you just don't worry about the season. You just worry about game to game."

Now, let's clarify something here: This is a sport in which chasing individual stats doesn't necessarily translate to not being a team guy. Baseball is an individual pursuit, especially that mano-a-mano battle between hitter and pitcher. For the most part the pursuit of a .300 batting average or 40 home runs or 200 hits usually contributes to winning rather than detracting from it.

And give Mookie credit for honesty, because a day after making those comments, he acknowledged that he wants to be in the Hall of Fame someday – like, who doesn't? – and "you have to accept these numbers are always going to be there. It's kind of hard to accept that. But at the end of the day, it is what it is. I just have to find ways to help the team win."

Sunday, he did so, dramatically breaking a tie the Padres had created in the top of the eighth. Asked afterward if he got any clarity from this approach, if maybe it freed him up to do damage on Suarez's 2-and-0 four-seamer, he said, "Every at-bat's the same at this point. You're just trying to do something productive. So it definitely helps, not carrying burdens from previous at-bats.

"... I finally did something good for the boys.

That's what the bat means. I've done a decent job with the glove, but (with) the bat, I really haven't done much, so it's just good to help."

Before Sunday's game, Dodgers manager Dave Roberts talked about "team at-bats," and it's quite possible that the urgency he wanted to see from his team this weekend – and did see – might have manifested itself in a hitter maybe giving himself up or altering his approach.

"My ask is to just be a better hitter, to fight and to, you know, put together (good) at-bats, and that's pretty much in any player's control, versus trying to hit a certain amount of homers or whatever, ribbies or this or that," he said, then noted that the urgency of a close race might demand more of those situational at-bats than a breeze to the wire, as has happened in other seasons.

"We've done it where you have a big lead and then you can kind of coast," he said. "And guys are kind of trying to cement their numbers or their seasons or whatever.

"But now when you're in (a tight race), you've got to win baseball games, right? And so it comes with more sacrifice. Whether it's a (sacrifice bunt) here or getting a guy over, a sacrifice fly, shortening up on the bat, winning (individual) pitches ... I kind of default to that type of play all the time. That's who I was as a ball player. So I see no downside in playing that type of baseball."

As for Betts, it's worth noting that in the last 11 games, dating to Aug. 5, his slash line is .340/.413/.522, with two homers, nine RBIs and 12 runs scored.

"Mookie's been very good for a couple of weeks now," said first baseman Freddie Freeman, whose own three-run homer in the first inning off of Yu Darvish got things rolling. "That was huge. A 2-0 fastball, he's able to stay through it, backspin the ball, hit it over the fence in a big situation. It's saying it all.

"The last few weeks. Mookie Betts is going to be Mookie Betts, and no one in here is worried about him. So it's good to see him get some results."

Others can benefit from that sort of mindset, and left fielder Michael Conforto, whose numbers (.191/.301/.328) are even more sickly, might be another of those guys convinced to abandon the season-long numerical goals and concentrate on situational at-bats.

"I would say it's actually freeing, in the sense of you're not expecting to put up a certain OPS or this or that," Roberts said. "You're just trying to help the team win."

And maybe, in the case of the star accustomed to pursuing and getting the big numbers, it's almost liberating to take that different approach.

"Just to take the pressure off, trying to recover from the (first part of) the season and kind of get more micro and just game-to-game and at-bat to at-bat," Roberts said. "It's just easier, a better quality of life. And certainly we're seeing the performance from Mookie."

If it continues and helps propel the Dodgers down the stretch, his numbers from the first 5½ months will be easily forgotten. ■

'I Think It's the Right Time'

Dodgers' Legend Clayton Kershaw Retiring After 2025 Season

By Bill Plunkett | September 18, 2025

One of the greatest left-handed pitchers of all-time has decided his time is up.

Dodgers pitching great Clayton Kershaw made it official Thursday, announcing that he will retire at the end of the 2025 season.

"I'm going to call it. I'm going to retire," Kershaw said at a press conference before Thursday's game at Dodger Stadium. "We talked about it a lot. Ellen (his wife) and I talked about it a lot. The kiddos talked about it a lot.

"I'm at peace with it. I think it's the right time."

The 37-year-old Kershaw is scheduled to make his final regular-season start at Dodger Stadium – where he has recorded 117 of his 222 career wins and notched his 3,000th career strikeout earlier this season – on Friday night against the San Francisco Giants. Depending on the length of the Dodgers' postseason run, it could be his final start at Dodger Stadium.

Kershaw acknowledged he and Ellen – who is pregnant with their fifth child – had adopted a year-to-year approach for a while now, waiting until the offseason to make a decision on continuing his career. This year was different.

"I think almost going into the season we kind of knew that this was going to be it," he said. "(But) I didn't want to say anything in case I changed my mind."

Coming back from last year's foot and knee surgeries and finishing this season both healthy and pitching well (he is 10-2 with a 3.53 ERA in 20 starts) made the decision easier. It was Ellen who pushed him to make it public before a final start at Dodger Stadium – anticipating the uncertainty of the postseason.

"I think just with this last home start coming up, I just felt it was the right time," he said. "Honestly Ellen had a lot to do with it. She kind of talked to me, and it just felt like everything had come together. Obviously we have another month to play and we have a lot of great pitchers, so everybody's role is kind of up in the air at this point. So I just didn't want this opportunity to pass by. It just kind of felt like the right thing to do."

In his comments Thursday, Kershaw thanked the Dodgers' organization, the training staff and coaches, then got choked up and shed some tears when speaking about his family and his teammates. Virtually the entire roster, along with Dodgers manager Dave Roberts, pitching coach Mark Prior, President of Baseball Operations Andrew Friedman, team president and CEO Stan Kasten and Executive VP Lon Rosen, crowded into the press conference room.

"The hardest one is the teammates, so I'm not even going to look at you guys in the eye," Kershaw said. "You guys sitting in this room, you mean so much to me. We have so much fun. I'm going to miss it. I'm going to miss working out Day One in the weight room, listening to crazy music with you guys, 'Shirtless Sundays' – I'm going to miss all of that. I'm going to miss the flights. I'm going to miss everything about them.

"The game itself, I'm going to miss a lot, but I'll be okay without that. I think the hard part is the feeling after a win, celebrating with you guys. That's pretty special."

Clayton Kershaw waves to the crowd after being taken out of the game in the fifth inning against the rival San Francisco Giants. (Los Angeles Daily News: Keith Birmingham)

DODGERS.COM
Dodgers
22

Roberts said Kershaw had told him about his retirement plans "a couple weeks ago" and told him Wednesday that he was going to announce it. Some of his teammates knew as well and Kershaw told everyone in the players' group text Thursday morning – asking them not to make it "weird."

"I've already got a jersey signed from him. Yeah, I've known," first baseman Freddie Freeman said. "But he told me to keep it a secret. He wanted to do it on his own terms. I didn't know when he was going to do it. And I think knowing Clayton, I thought he would just not even tell anybody and just retire. But I'm glad he did. So the fans, and not only Dodger fans, but all baseball fans can enjoy his last start here at Dodger Stadium in the regular season tomorrow.

"He's not a Dodger legend. He's a baseball legend forever. I mean, the greatest pitcher of our generation."

There were signs that Kershaw had entered his "Last Dance" phase this season. He embraced the fans and celebrated his 3,000th strikeout more openly than previous milestones. Chosen as the Legacy Pick for the All-Star Game, he agreed to be mic'd up during his one inning on the mound – very out of character for Kershaw, who is notoriously prickly even to teammates on his start days.

"I know he's saying it and I know it's kind of the reality, but I still don't know if I believe it," third baseman Max Muncy said. "For as long as I've been here, it's been 22 (Kershaw's jersey number)."

The three-time National League Cy Young Award winner has played all 18 of his major-league seasons with the Dodgers since they selected him seventh overall in the 2006 MLB Draft. His 222-96 record and 15 shutouts rank first among active major-league pitchers.

Kershaw will finish his career as an 11-time All-Star who won the 2014 National League MVP award and three Cy Youngs. He is one of just 11 pitchers in MLB history to win both the Cy Young and MVP awards in the same season and his 2.54 ERA is the lowest of any pitcher in the live-ball era (since 1920). His winning percentage tops all pitchers with at least 200 victories since 1900.

Most crucially, he has been part of two World Series championship teams, 2020 and 2024 (though he did not pitch last October due to his chronic foot injury), after being criticized for his postseason failures in previous seasons – often while pitching on short rest or coming on in relief.

"For me, the unselfish ability he's had in the past, where, when the postseason came, he would take the ball when it was his turn, and he would also take the ball when it wasn't his turn, coming out of the 'pen, doing anything the team asked of him," Muncy said. "He never said, 'No.' He never said his arm hurts, he never said 'I need a little more time.' It was 'Whatever this team needs to get over the hump, I'm gonna do it.'

"You're talking about one of the best pitchers of all time, and for him to be that unselfish is pretty ridiculous."

Kershaw's career can be broken into two parts. Through 2017, he had finished in the top five in NL Cy Young voting seven times, winning it in 2011, 2013 and 2014. He pitched a no-hitter on June 18, 2014. But recurring back injuries became an annual challenge and injuries characterized the second half of his career. He returned following shoulder, knee and foot surgeries the past two offseasons.

He opened each of the past two seasons on the injured list. In 2024, Kershaw was forced to end his season in August because of a chronic toe injury that limited him to seven starts and just 30 innings with a 2-2 record and a 4.50 ERA, all career lows.

He missed the entire postseason, including the Dodgers' World Series victory over the New York Yankees. This season, he didn't make his first start until May. Adapting to diminished velocity on his fastball, Kershaw has gone 10-2 with a 3.53 ERA in 20 starts with the Dodgers carefully tempering his workload.

"He definitely has a lot more," Freeman said. "I think he could keep going for a couple more years if he really wanted to. Guys that get to first base still go, 'I cannot see the slider.' And then he throws a 71, 72 mph curveball. I know he's not throwing 94, 95 like when I was facing him anymore. But he still knows how to pitch. He's the best to ever do it."

Considered a lock to be a first-ballot Hall of Famer, Kershaw will be eligible for Cooperstown in 2031.

Clayton Kershaw announced in September that 2025 would be his final season in Major League Baseball. (Los Angeles Daily News: David Crane)

STARTING PITCHER

22 CLAYTON KERSHAW

This 'Kershaw Day' Was a Celebration

By Jim Alexander | September 20, 2025

By the end, was there any emotion left?

Friday in Los Angeles was, barring a Clayton Kershaw postseason appearance in The Ravine, the last home game to be celebrated as "Kershaw Day." That's been the way Dodger fans have marked time over most of the last 18 seasons, the implication being that on any day the ace was scheduled to take the mound, life held unimaginable promise.

Even if he was no longer unquestionably the ace.

At 37 his stuff is diminished, and as the late Don Sutton used to put it, he is instead dazzling 'em with his footwork. And though Kershaw often has pitched with clinical effectiveness in 2025 – and was, for a change, healthy late in a season – there seems to be uncertainty over the role he'll assume in the postseason, on a starting staff that is both healthy and loaded.

The reaction in Dodger Stadium on Friday night, all the way through his 4⅓-inning, 91-pitch outing in a 6-3 victory over the San Francisco Giants, wasn't so much "farewell" as it was "thank you." Thanks for the memories, thanks for the triumphs, thanks for conducting your career with class and for going out in the same way.

And he responded in kind, right from the beginning of the night – when his teammates held back as he ran to the mound so he could soak in the crowd's affection, before he noticed he was the only one out there and frantically waved at them to join him on the field.

"I didn't love it, but it was a great gesture," he said. "You know, the guys have gone above and beyond the last few days for me. ... I never want to (be) a distraction to the game or anything like that, because obviously winning is the most important thing for us, especially right now.

"The whole night was just special."

About the only thing Kershaw didn't come away with Friday night was a victory, and maybe this was a case of going out the way he came in. When he first reached the majors in May of 2008, as a 20-year-old prospect who had been impressive in Double-A, it took 10 appearances (plus another brief sojourn in the minors) before he posted his first big league pitching victory, a 2-0 victory over the Washington Nationals on July 27, 2008.

This season, in 21 starts, he has a 10-2 record and 3.55 ERA, and has won his last six decisions. Friday's was a no-decision because he left after getting Rafael Devers on a called third strike for the first out of the fifth, on his 91st pitch of the night. He left with a 2-1 deficit, and the game ball, but Edgardo Henriquez was the subsequent beneficiary of Shohei Ohtani's three-run homer and Mookie Betts' solo shot in the bottom of the inning, for a 5-2 Dodger lead.

But when Manager Dave Roberts came out to

Clayton Kershaw waves to the crowd after being taken out of the game in the fifth inning against the rival San Francisco Giants. (Los Angeles Daily News: Keith Birmingham)

Dodgers
22
Coca-Cola
22

replace him, he also gave Kershaw a hug on the mound as the crowd – announced as 53,037, ticket prices on the secondary market having spiked for this last home appearance – gave him a standing ovation. Kershaw doffed his cap, crossed his arms as if to give the entire crowd a hug, embraced his teammates one by one, popped back out of the dugout and tapped his heart, and waved to his wife Ellen and family in the second deck.

Were there tears shed?

"From him, yes," Roberts said.

Part of the reason for this emotion, and this celebration? Performance, obviously; three Cy Young Awards, an MVP trophy, more than 3,000 strikeouts and two World Series rings sort of speak for themselves.

And another part involved longevity and loyalty. A meme on social media noted three players who approached 20-year careers exclusively in L.A.: Kershaw, the late Kobe Bryant with the Lakers and the Kings' Anze Kopitar, who announced that this would be his final season just a couple of hours before Kershaw made his retirement official on Thursday afternoon.

Kershaw said at last year's World Series celebration that he was a "Dodger for life." This cemented it, and the fans of L.A. obviously have relished it.

"I don't think it can (be overstated), in a world (where) people take the easy way out, chase short money," Roberts said before the game. "You know, the 'grass is greener' kind of adage. The loyalty part of it is just not what it used to be. That's just my opinion.

"Clayton lives by those values, and it means something for him to wear the same uniform. And was it rocky, was it uneasy at the negotiating table at times, and taking a little bit less, or betting on yourself or whatever it might be to remain a Dodger? Yeah, but I think for me that's where I just gained a lot of respect for him."

The fans have as well. Kershaw compared it to a relationship, noting that "You've been 18 years in this with them, and there's some great times. And then, you know, there's some times where you probably want to break up for a minute. I think just having them behind me the way they have been has been it's just been icing on the cake."

Even Kershaw's fatal flaw, all of those postseasons when he came up empty, will be only a small blemish on his resume. Winning two rings in the last five seasons has helped, and he does have a chance at another in 2025. And it must be noted that many of those postseason issues arose in situations when he had to pitch on short rest or longer into games, to assume a greater workload because others couldn't.

He was willing to "take on the responsibility, the burden of being, you know, the clear-cut staff ace and what had to come with that, right?" Roberts said. "He's kind of seen the organization where it was, and there were some lean times 18 years ago. To then kind of see where we're at the last 10, 12 years ... he's been right there in the middle of it."

That's your reminder, by the way, that Kershaw broke in with the Frank McCourt Dodgers. This franchise has come a long way in 18 years, just as he has.

"I'm so grateful I got to be here so long," Kershaw said. "We've had a lot of great teams throughout the years, and we have a lot of great people come through those doors. And the Dodger culture has been established long before me, and it'll be established long after I'm gone.

"You know, that's the cool thing about baseball is that your career will just be gone in an instant, and the game keeps going ... this game doesn't need anybody, you know? So I'm just, I'm so grateful I got to be a small part of Dodger history for as long as I've been here. We've had some amazing groups along the way. And this one's pretty special this year."

There will be one last regular-season start next weekend in Seattle followed by another playoff run, this one with the deepest starting rotation this franchise has carried into a postseason in decades.

And let it be noted that the guy who has worn 22 all these years – all but that first game in 2008, when the rookie callup wore No. 54 – is currently sitting on 222 career victories. If he's the last Dodger to wear No. 22 before it goes up on the left field facade and Kershaw himself heads for Cooperstown, that would probably be fitting.

In the meantime, what will the fans do to replace "Kershaw Day?" ■

Clayton Kershaw carried the mantle of "ace" for much of his 18-year tenure with the Dodgers and proved willing to shoulder the responsibility that came with it. (Los Angeles Daily News: Keith Birmingham)

CUTWATER®
6:12
BANK OF AMERICA
360
76
Dodgers
blu
calif

WELCOME TO D
Booking.com
WILD CARD

NLWC

Los Angeles Daily News: Keith Birmingham

National League Wild Card Game 1
September 30, 2025 | Los Angeles, California
DODGERS 10, REDS 5

Double-Double

Shohei Ohtani and Teoscar Hernandez Each Homer Twice in Rout of Reds

By Bill Plunkett

That had to be more fun than a sim game.

Forced by their two-month dawdle during the regular season to open the postseason in action instead of finding ways to occupy their time for five days, the Dodgers treated the Cincinnati Reds like simulated opponents in Game 1 of their Wild Card Series.

Shohei Ohtani and Teoscar Hernandez each hit two home runs, Tommy Edman hit one – tying the Dodgers' postseason franchise record and threatening a serious seed shortage – and Blake Snell took a shutout into the seventh inning of a 10-5 victory.

"We were talking about it pregame, we gotta establish our presence and really make our mark on this game early," Edman said. "We did a good job of that today."

Evan Phillips on supporting team during playoffs

There were a different set of marks late.

Clouds gathered when Snell left the game, though. Handed an eight-run lead in the eighth inning, the Dodgers' bullpen struggled to get the final six outs – a performance the Dodgers can only hope is not a foreshadowing of postseason problems to come.

The Dodgers will go for the quick knockout of the Reds on Wednesday night with Yoshinobu Yamamoto scheduled to start Game 2 of the best-of-three series.

Whatever puncher's chance the Reds had depended on getting a dominant start from Hunter Greene in Game 1. That disappeared over the right-field wall quickly enough.

Ohtani turned around a 100.4 mph fastball from Greene in the first inning – the fastest pitch Ohtani has hit for a home run during his MLB career (regular season or postseason) – and sent it on a line into the right field pavilion at 117.7 mph.

"It was a really hard pitch to hit, but I felt like I reacted pretty well," Ohtani understated through his interpreter. "I was happy I was able to help the team score early."

It was the second-highest combination of velocity coming in and going out recorded during the Statcast Era (2015) – behind Ohtani's 120 mph home run off Pirates rookie Bubba Chandler's 99.2 mph fastball earlier this month – and the hardest-hit home run off a 100-plus mph pitch since 2015 as well.

"We said it before the game, 'We want to come out and make a statement.' Shohei definitely did that," Dodgers catcher Ben Rortvedt said.

"It's crazy, but it's easy to take it for granted when it happens so often. I feel like I'm clapping as if someone gets another hit. It's right after I hit, too, so I'm sitting down, taking my stuff off. I can barely see, and I see him rounding home plate. It's awesome."

Greene's night only got worse in the third inning. The former Sherman Oaks Notre Dame High star walked back-to-back batters, threw a wild pitch to move them up, then hung a slider to Teoscar Hernandez. Hernandez sent it into the left-field pavilion for a three-run home run.

Two pitches later, Greene left another slider belt high on the inside corner to Edman. He deposited that one over the right-field wall for back-to-back homers.

Two batters later, Greene's night was done and Game 1 of the WCS was looking like an extension of the late August series when the Dodgers outscored the Reds 18-4 in a three-game sweep.

Teoscar Hernandez hit his second home run of the night in the fifth inning. Ohtani hit his second of the night in the sixth inning, a two-run home run just as impressive as the first. It left his bat at 113.5 mph and traveled 454 feet into the upper reaches of the right-field pavilion.

"His focus gets more keen and the at-bat quality is better," Dodgers manager Dave Roberts said of Ohtani's postseason personality. "That's the reason why he signed to be with this ballclub, this organization, to play in games like this to showcase his other-worldly talent. I expect really fun things this postseason out of Shohei."

The five-homer barrage of the Reds tied the franchise record for home runs in a postseason game set in Game 3 of the 2020 National League Championship Series against the Atlanta Braves and matched in Game 5 of the 2021 NLCS also against the Braves.

Snell gave the Reds nothing to cling to for hope when they left the ballpark.

Facing the Reds for the first time since he no-hit them last August, Snell was dominant for six scoreless innings - and pleasingly efficient for a Dodgers team hoping to limit its bullpen exposure on a nightly basis. He needed just 70 pitches to get through the first six innings and gave up just one hit in that time while striking out nine.

"I mean, you could see the obvious stuff - like power to the fastball, velocity in the upper 90s, spins the ball," Reds manager Terry Francona said. "I thought the big difference-maker was his changeup - it was his ability to manipulate the changeup, like even vary it. He'd throw one that was 87 (mph) and one that was 82 off the first changeup. And he threw multiple - like, two, three, four in a row at times and all different speeds. And then you throw a 97 (mph fastball) in there, and it becomes difficult."

The Reds did get to him for two runs in the seventh inning. But Snell left with a six-run lead. Even when that lead grew to eight runs before the eighth inning, the Dodgers' bullpen made it uncomfortable.

Alex Vesia retired just one of the three batters he faced and Edgardo Henriquez none. Jack Dreyer followed with the fourth walk of the inning before getting the final outs of a three-run eighth. It took 59 pitches for the trio of relievers to get three outs.

"Alex wasn't sharp tonight. And obviously Henriquez didn't have any command," Roberts said. "You follow up in a 10-2 ball game with Edgardo in a lane that I feel very confident in, and he just wasn't good tonight.

"It's very clear to me, when you're on the attack, those guys (the Reds) are on their heels with the lead we have. When you start being too fine and getting behind, you start giving them free bases and that's how you can build innings and get momentum. So that's what I saw in that inning there for sure."

Blake Treinen closed it out with no more drama in the ninth. ■

National League Wild Card Game 2
October 1, 2025 | Los Angeles, California
DODGERS 8, REDS 4

Ready to Roll

Mookie Betts Drives in Three Runs as Dodgers Advance to NLDS

By Bill Plunkett

Shock treatment can be effective in extreme cases.

Something about those back-to-back walk-off losses at Camden Yards in early September got the Dodgers' attention and awakened the defending champions. They have won 17 of 22 games since then, including two in a row over the Cincinnati Reds to sweep their Wild Card Series.

They spotted the Reds a two-run head-start but came roaring back to win, 8-4, in Game 2 and eliminate the Reds in quick order to move on to the next round of the postseason.

"I think we just knew we were getting close to October and we couldn't be making the mistakes we were making at that time," Teoscar Hernandez said of the stretch-run renaissance. "Concentration got bigger. Focus got bigger. And the little things come up. I think that's what has been the key to us winning the way we're winning."

The quick knockout of the Reds gives the Dodgers multiple options at starting pitcher for Game 1 against the Phillies – and they chose Shohei Ohtani. He did not pitch in the Wild Card Series and Dodgers manager Dave Roberts announced the choice following Game 2.

But the Dodgers couldn't escape town without another reminder of the baggage their bullpen is carrying. The Reds scored twice in the eighth inning with Emmet Sheehan – one of starters moved to the bullpen to stabilize things – walking two, throwing a wild pitch and retiring just one of the five batters he faced.

But Roki Sasaki continues to be a revelation in a bullpen role, setting things right with a 1-2-3 ninth inning that included two strikeouts.

"Wow. That's really all you can say is wow," third baseman Max Muncy said of Sasaki's finish. "That's what we need right there."

With all the focus on the bullpen's ability to derail the Dodgers' postseason, another problem was forgotten – poor outfield defense.

Teoscar Hernandez provided a reminder in the first inning. Dodgers starter Yoshinobu Yamamoto hit Spencer Steer with a pitch but was heading for the dugout when he got Austin Hays to pop up into shallow right field near the foul line.

Hernandez came jogging in to make the play but took his eye off the ball and dropped it. Six pitches later, the next batter, Sal Stewart, slapped a two-out, two-run single into right field to get the Reds on the scoreboard first.

"I felt terrible," Hernandez said. "We knew we had Yama on the mound and we wanted to give him the best chance to go deeper in the game then I made him throw some more pitches that he wasn't supposed to throw in that first inning. But at the same time, it's part of the game. I don't want to make those mistakes, especially now in October. But I just have to try to be better next time."

The bottom of the Dodgers' lineup atoned for Hernandez's sin.

Ben Rortvedt led off the third inning by slicing a double into left field, the first of two hits in the game for the Dodgers' No. 9 hitter. He moved up on a ground out and scored on Mookie Betts' RBI single – one of

Betts' four hits, the other three doubles (tying the franchise postseason record for a one game).

Two innings later, the Dodgers grabbed the lead on Kiké Hernandez's RBI double and Miguel Rojas' RBI single.

The bottom three hitters in the Dodgers' order – Hernandez, Rojas and Rortvedt – finished the night 6 for 12 with five runs scored.

"I think what we're seeing is winning pitches, using the whole field, fighting and not trying to just slug. I think we're taking team at-bats," Roberts said of an offense that put up 18 runs in two games against the Reds.

"Situationally, we've been fantastic, and even Rort at the bottom, whether it's a sacrifice, the fight to slap an 0-2 double the other way to get on base. We're doing whatever it takes, whether it's a sac fly – even Shohei in a situation, getting a guy over to set the stage for Mookie. Just team baseball. Team at-bats."

It was still a one-run game when Yamamoto ran into trouble in the top of the sixth. Three singles loaded the bases with no outs.

The Reds came away empty-handed when Yamamoto got Austin Hays to bounce into a force out at home then struck out Stewart and Elly De La Cruz, each finished off by a curveball from Yamamoto.

The curveball was a critical weapon for Yamamoto against the Reds. He got seven of his 17 swings-and-misses with it.

That work pushed Yamamoto's pitch count up to 95, though, and the countdown was on to see how much the Dodgers' unreliable bullpen would have to be asked to get. A four-run bottom of the sixth made that question less compelling.

Again, the bottom of the Dodgers' order lit the fire. Kiké Hernandez singled and Rortvedt reached on an error by Stewart at first base. Ohtani drove in one run with a single and Betts another with a double.

After the Reds intentionally walked Freddie Freeman, Teoscar Hernandez made up for his error with a two-run single.

Roberts showed his true feelings about the bullpen by sending Yamamoto back out for the seventh inning. His first two walks of the night put two on with two outs when Roberts finally came to get him. Yamamoto threw a season-high 113 pitches in his 6⅔ innings.

It seemed to take just as many pitches to get the final seven outs. Sheehan walked two, threw a wild pitch, retired just one of the five batters he faced in the eighth and was yanked mid-at-bat by Roberts.

"It was his first kind of real crack at kind of late leverage," Roberts said. "He wasn't sharp, but I believe in him, I really do. And I think for me to think that he can get through (Will) Benson, although he had count leverage, to then feel like he can get through (Matt) McLain, he would have been over 30 pitches, I just didn't think his stuff was as sharp.

"For me, I just had a gut feeling that, give (Alex) Vesia a chance to get leverage versus (Miguel) Andujar or if they leave Benson in. And I liked him against McLain and (T.J.) Freidl. And that's my thought."

Alex Vesia struck out Benson but walked McLain to load the bases before he struck out Friedl.

"Doc made a call. He was trusting his gut," Vesia said. "And I definitely think that it paid off. Doc's a legend, man, and that's the (stuff) that legends do right there."

Sasaki handled the ninth with the renewed confidence and overpowering pitch mix he has shown since moving to the bullpen.

"I trust him, and he's going to be pitching in leverage," Roberts said when asked if Sasaki could be the answer to his bullpen's problems. "I don't think the moment's going to be too big for Roki." ■

RELIEF/STARTING PITCHER

11

ROKI SASAKI

Roki Sasaki Looks Like a Solution for Dodgers' Biggest Weakness

By Bill Plunkett | October 2, 2025

For most of his rookie season, Roki Sasaki's biggest impact on the Dodgers was his off-hand remark to team president Stan Kasten during his free-agency recruiting visit that led to the team adding high-tech, Japanese-style toilets to the renovated clubhouse.

Now, Sasaki could be the difference between the Dodgers getting flushed out of the playoffs short of their goal or solving the biggest threat to their title defense.

"I think he's really helpful. Really talented," Dodgers president of baseball operations Andrew Friedman said after Sasaki's latest electric relief appearance closed out the Cincinnati Reds in the Wild Card Series on Wednesday night. "He can get out righties and lefties. So obviously he's really helpful."

Helpful? Like a fire hose is helpful in putting out a fire? While relievers that have been taking the ball all season have fallen off Dodgers manager Dave Roberts' "trust tree" like fall leaves dropping, Sasaki has arrived on the scene as the kind of dynamic bullpen weapon that can transform a postseason.

"I just feel like he wants the ball and everybody else should feel the same way," veteran infielder Miguel Rojas said.

"Roki has been setting the bar really, really high for everybody else because he wants to pitch and everybody else should feel the same way. It doesn't matter what the score is. You've got to come in and attack hitters and be careless about what's happening. If you give up a run, we have an offense that can respond back and we showed it tonight (in Game 2 against the Reds). We showed it last night. And we've been showing it for a couple weeks now."

Rojas hints at the "crisis of confidence" that Roberts has pegged as the main factor in the struggles of the Dodgers' bullpen. Friedman agrees with that assessment – and that Sasaki can turn it around.

"We've talked about this – I don't think our bullpen struggles are talent-related. It's execution," Friedman said. "We see it with walking guys and getting behind in counts, which to me comes from confidence. So we have to figure out a way to spark that and if Roki's outing tonight is that spark, it wouldn't surprise me."

A month ago, it would have been a dubious thought.

"I don't remember exactly when the delivery stuff clicked," Friedman said. "Before that, no. After that, yeah."

Sasaki started the season in the Dodgers' starting rotation. For eight starts, he struggled with his command and looked nothing like the dynamic pitcher so many teams pursued last winter. He went to the injured list in May with a shoulder injury that was a factor in his final season in Japan as well.

A move to the bullpen helped salvage what was looking like a lost 2025 season for Roki Sasaki. (Los Angeles Daily News: Keith Birmingham)

LA
FERNANDO
34
LA

When his shoulder finally felt healthy enough to start a rehab assignment with Triple-A Oklahoma City in mid-August, the results were not good. He continued to struggle with his command and hitters were unimpressed by a fastball that had lost the 100-mph sizzle it had in Japan.

In early September, the Dodgers used a minor calf injury as an excuse to extend Sasaki's rehab time in Triple-A but also sent him to their training complex in Arizona to work with their director of pitching Rob Hill. Sasaki worked on using the lower half of his body to drive his mechanics and keeping his shoulders aligned properly.

That time seems to have provided a breakthrough. Sasaki emerged with his top-tier velocity restored. Confidence has followed.

"Roki has kind of been on his own trying to get his feels and things like that. But he and Rob had a really good session and tapped into some velocity," Roberts said at the time.

"I think a lot of young, talented players just out-talent leagues and they don't really need to make any type of adjustments. It happens with Americans, it happens with pitchers, with position players with a lot of young players. I just think it was something where he needed some suggestions for guidance and Rob was there and it worked out well."

Friedman said the Dodgers' coaches needed time for Sasaki to trust them and adopt the changes they suggested.

"We didn't try to push it too early. We knew that he was a guy that was accustomed to doing things a certain way and we were going to embrace that," Friedman said. "At the same time, forging a relationship and building trust and getting to a place where we could partner together and not pushing it prematurely.

"His delivery had gotten out of whack. The compensation for the oblique injury (during his 2024 season in Japan) and then obviously it led to some shoulder soreness. So just getting him feeling right and then syncing up his body again was really important and he was all-in obviously on doing that. It's just how to get from A to B. Connor McGuiness, Mark Prior, Rob Hill have done an unbelievable job with him and the way he worked coming back made for a really devastating combo in terms of getting him back to the point of what we saw tonight (in WCS Game 2)."

Sasaki had never pitched in relief as a professional before making two appearances out of the bullpen for OKC before he was activated from the IL. He made two appearances out of the Dodgers' bullpen before the end of the regular season and then his postseason debut Wednesday night.

Sasaki has retired nine of the 10 batters he has faced in relief, six on strikeouts. The Dodgers have simplified his pitch mix. Since returning he has thrown only four-seam fastballs or splitters. He needed just 11 pitches to dismiss the Reds in the ninth inning on Wednesday, four splitters and seven fastballs that ranged from 99.8 mph to 101.4 mph.

"You guys see it – when you've got to gear up for 101, then you've got to hit a splitter like his? I'm glad I'm catching him," Ben Rortvedt said.

"That guy is gross," fellow reliever Tanner Scott said. "That guy is gross."

The combination of good health, improved mechanics and the confidence that has come with success have given the Dodgers "the 2023 version of Roki," Friedman said.

Roberts and Friedman both backed away from naming Sasaki their closer – let alone the savior that many fans and observers have anointed him. And there are still questions about how much of a workload he can take on as a reliever. But he has already added a dash of hope to the Dodgers' bullpen outlook.

"We don't know yet," Friedman said of how often Sasaki can be deployed, a problem mitigated by the extra day off in this year's National League Division Series schedule. "We used him two out of three (days) and he rebounded from that well. Beyond that, we don't know yet.

"He's going to get important outs for us. I don't know when." ■

While Roki Sasaki will likely get a shot to start again in the future, his overpowering pitching was just what the Dodgers needed in the postseason. (Los Angeles Daily News: Keith Birmingham)

Dodgers
11
Capital One

NLDS

Los Angeles Daily News: Keith Birmingham

National League Division Series Game 1
October 4, 2025 | Philadelphia, Pennsylvania
DODGERS 5, PHILLIES 3

All is Forgiven

Teoscar Hernandez Makes Up for an Early Defensive Gaffe with a Go-Ahead Three-Run Home Run in Game 1

By Bill Plunkett

Like a guilty husband bringing home flowers in hopes of escaping the doghouse, Teoscar Hernandez made up for his transgression with an even better gift.

Hernandez's poor effort on defense cost the Dodgers a run. That run looked like it might be the difference in Game 1 of their National League Division Series with the Philadelphia Phillies – until Hernandez produced a go-ahead three-run home run in the seventh inning that brought the Dodgers a 5-3 comeback win on Saturday night.

The best-of-five series will go dark on Sunday – the Super Bowl champion Eagles are hosting the Denver Broncos across the street at Lincoln Financial Field, tush-pushing the MLB playoffs out of the neighborhood.

They came back despite Shohei Ohtani giving up three runs in six innings in his postseason pitching debut – the first runs he has allowed since August – while striking out four times at the plate.

"I'm going to give the credit to our hitting coach," veteran infielder Miguel Rojas said of the comeback win. "He called it earlier when we had the (hitters) meeting today. Aaron Bates said something to us, that it's going to be there. The intensity and the fans were going to be there early in the game. Obviously they scored early. They punched us in the face right there. But we knew we were going to be winning in the seventh inning. He said it.

"He said that we were going to have an opportunity to come back in the game and it happened."

Citizens Bank Park was rocking alright – on Wednesday night. The Phillies held an intrasquad scrimmage, trying to stave off the staleness of a five-day break and invited their fans. That became a very well-attended practice – practice? – when 31,000 showed up.

The atmosphere was even better Saturday. A sellout crowd made plenty of noise without Dr. Ken screaming at them from the scoreboard or the speaker volume threatening to put another crack in the Liberty Bell.

The Phillies responded by getting to Ohtani for those three runs in the second inning.

Ohtani lit the fuse by walking Alec Bohm to start the inning then gave up a single to Brandon Marsh – the Phillies' first hit after six no-hit innings against Ohtani (five in his September start against them).

Both runners scored when J.T. Realmuto lined a triple into the right-center field gap. The ball went to the wall – but it shouldn't have. Right fielder Teoscar Hernandez's lackluster effort at cutting the ball off led to a third run when Realmuto scored from third on Harrison Bader's sacrifice fly.

Teoscar Hernandez launches a go-ahead three-run home run to give the Dodgers the lead for good in Game 1. (AP Images)

Dodgers
37

"I was playing straight in. I didn't get a good angle," Teoscar Hernandez said. "He hit it pretty good. I tried to get it, so he can't go all the way to third or they can score two runs in that situation. It went by me."

Dodgers manager Dave Roberts defended Hernandez's defense by saying "he wasn't not trying" but admitted "Yeah, that's a ball that you don't want Realmuto to have a triple."

Ohtani allowed just one more hit in six innings and held the Phillies' dangerous duo of Kyle Schwarber and Bryce Harper hitless in six at-bats against him, including four strikeouts.

"Prior to the game, just preparing for the game, just looking at the data, doing my usual preparation – I was a little nervous imagining myself out there on the mound," Ohtani said through his interpreter. "But once I was on the mound and on the field, that went away and it was really me focusing."

Hernandez's faulty throttle was the difference when the Dodgers finally got to Sanchez in the sixth inning.

Tommy Edman singled to put two runners on for Kiké Hernandez who did what he does in October, coming through with a clutch hit. He drove in two with a double down the left field line, Edman roaring through third base coach Dino Ebel's "stop" sign to score.

"It broke the seal," Bates said. "And once you break that seal, it kind of opens the door for the rest of the guys. ... You're always kind of waiting for that big hit. And he got it with that double."

Kiké Hernandez's double did more than wake up the offense. It also drove Sanchez from the game.

With veteran setup man David Robertson on the mound in the seventh, Pages led off with a single and Robertson clipped Will Smith with a pitch to put two runners on.

Left-hander Matt Strahm came in and struck out Ohtani – Ohtani's fourth strikeout of the game, the third on a called third strike.

"They have really quality arms coming out of the Phillies starting pitcher and bullpen," Ohtani said. "And the fact that when I'm leading off, it does allow for the bullpen, the left-handed (relievers) bullpen to come out. That really gives Mookie and Teo, hitting behind me the opportunity to be able to hit. So in that sense, I felt like even though the results weren't good, that I was able to contribute."

At one point this season, the Dodgers started batting Teoscar Hernandez ahead of Freeman against left-handed pitching. Roberts called it the "Teo tax" – opposing managers who brought in lefties to face Ohtani would have to leave them in to face both Betts and Hernandez if they also wanted the left-on-left matchup against Freeman.

Strahm got Betts to pop out but then the tax came due. Strahm's 91.8 mph fastball to Hernandez caught too much of the plate. Hernandez lined it into the right field seats for his fourth home run in three postseason games – and 394 feet of restitution.

"I watched videos. He likes to go up in the strike zone. I think that's when he's stronger," Teoscar Hernandez said. "My first three at-bats (all strikeouts), I chased a lot of down.

"Not trying to overswing or anything like that. Maybe a hit. Try to bring in one run to tie the game. But he left it over the strike zone."

That left nine outs for the Dodgers' bullpen to get with a two-run lead – a tall task for the old bullpen but maybe not so much with the reconfigured group. Tyler Glasnow got the first five but handed the ball off to Alex Vesia with the bases loaded in the eighth. Vesia got pinch-hitter Edmundo Sosa to fly out and squash that threat.

Roki Sasaki got the ball in the ninth – his second ninth-inning appearance in the past two games but his first in a save situation. He gave up a one-out double to Max Kepler but closed it out.

"Honestly, I could have gone to a couple other guys in those spots," Roberts said. "But just kind of knowing who I've got, I felt good about those guys we ran out there." ■

Shohei Ohtani made a strong postseason debut as a starting pitcher for the Dodgers going six innings, giving up three earned runs and striking out nine while picking up the win. (AP Images)

LA
Dodgers

MOOKIE BETTS

Mookie Betts' 'Failed' Season Turned Around Just in Time for Dodgers

By Bill Plunkett | October 5, 2025

Mookie Betts had doubts.

After all, a year ago, he had started the season as the Dodgers' shortstop but he didn't finish the season there. He moved back to right field after returning from a broken hand in August.

"(At) the start of the (2025) season I wasn't sure I would end the season there. I thought there may have to be adjustment at some point because from lack of trust or whatever," Betts said as the postseason started last week. "I just didn't know. I didn't know.

"I'm just proud of myself for making it all the way through the year and actually achieving a goal that I kind of set out to do, and that's being a major league shortstop, and say I did it and I'm good at it."

He is. Though he didn't often appear in highlights packages, he made all the plays a major-league shortstop is supposed to make – so much so that he led everyone at the position with 17 Defensive Runs Saved. He made just seven errors in 148 games – 19 shortstops made more.

Betts applied his elite-level work ethic to learning the position, putting in daily offseason work with Dodgers coach Chris Woodward, good friend Ryan Goins (Angels bench coach), and former Gold Glove shortstop Troy Tulowitzki. But Betts knew he had become a real shortstop when "I didn't have to think about it."

"I could just go out there and play," Betts said. "Now when I go out and play shortstop, it's like I'm going out to right field. I don't even think about it. My training is good. I believe in myself. I believe in what I can do. And now it's just like – go have fun. When the ball comes, have fun.

"I don't know when it happened, but there was just a point – I think it was probably after three or four errors, probably after three or four errors. I was making errors I never made before. I have never been in these situations. So once I got into the situation and understood how to do what I did wrong and understand how to do it (correctly) – just have fun."

Dodgers manager Dave Roberts saw the same change in Betts.

"There was a play – I don't recall where it was at – but a play going to his backhand that he made this play, pretty spectacular play, where, for me, it was just being an athlete playing shortstop and not just kind of the mechanical part of it," Roberts said, referencing a play against the Cincinnati Reds in late August.

"He just looked like a natural shortstop right

While Mookie Betts didn't have the year at the plate he envisioned, he put up a strong performance in his move back to shortstop. (Los Angeles Daily News: David Crane)

LA
Dodgers

there. I don't remember the backhand play, but then he's been as good as I could have ever expected playing that position."

But there were other doubts. For the first time in his big-league career, there were doubts about Betts' offense.

Many questioned whether the mental and physical effort Betts was putting into learning how to play shortstop was taking away from his offense.

Betts dismissed that theory and now admits what the real problem probably was. The virus that hit him near the end of spring training lingered longer than anyone expected, causing Betts to lose 20 pounds from a frame that is charitably listed at 5-foot-10, 180 pounds.

Once he shed the virus, Betts gained the weight back soon enough. But the loss of strength lasted much longer and led to swing changes that dragged Betts into the worst offensive slump of his career.

That was an even newer experience for Betts than playing shortstop. He had never had to deal with failure over such a sustained period and it led to frustration. After a game on Aug. 8, he declared his season over, accepting that the back of his baseball card would always reflect 2025 as "not a great season."

And then it was – at least for two months.

Freed from trying to save his season – and buoyed by a meeting with friend, hitting advisor and personal hype man J.D. Martinez – Betts started hitting like himself again. From that August night through the end of the season, he hit .309 with an .874 OPS, nine home runs and 34 RBIs in 45 games. He has started the postseason 6 for 14 with a four-hit game (including three doubles) in the closeout game of the Wild Card Series.

"It's just hard to gain your weight and sustain strength in the middle of a season, when you've been traveling and doing all these things," Betts said. "I think I finally got all that back and was able to fix a couple of mechanics and didn't really have to try and add on power anymore. I could just swing and let it do its thing."

When reminded of his "my season is kind of over" declaration in August, Betts said he "just accepted failing" and with that his mindset changed.

"My thought process on failing changed," he said. "Instead of looking at the things as failures, I looked at it as, OK, well, I know that's not it. Now I can move to the next thing. I know that's not it, move to the next thing, instead of sulking in – well, I tried this and it failed, now I don't know where to go. I just used it as positive and things eventually turned.

"But it's just one of those things where you've just gotta keep going, man. I went through arguably one of the worst years of my career. But I think it really made me mentally tough. So now there's just a different level of focus. And it's not really on myself; it's more on winning the game." ■

Mookie Betts persevered through a challenging season on and off the field to help lead the Dodgers to postseason success yet again. (Los Angeles Daily News: Keith Birmingham)

Dodgers
50
BETTS
Dodgers
SEASON 2025
NLDS
Booking.

National League Division Series Game 2

October 6, 2025 | Philadelphia, Pennsylvania

DODGERS 4, PHILLIES 3

Wheel and Deal

Roki Sasaki and Dodgers Defense Step Up in Tense Ninth Inning

By Bill Plunkett

Trapped in their recurring nightmare, the Dodgers woke up just in time.

In danger of blowing a four-run lead over the final two innings, the Dodgers came through with a game-saving defensive play and a game-closing reliever, holding on to beat the Philadelphia Phillies, 4-3, in Game 2 of their National League Division Series.

After beating the team with the best home record in baseball this season twice to start this series, the Dodgers head home needing just one more win to advance.

Ninety previous teams have gone up 2-0 in a best-of-five series (either in the NLDS or the old Championship Series format). Only 10 of them failed to advance.

"Yeah, we're in a great position, but they're not going to quit," Dodgers third baseman Max Muncy said. "You've heard me say it all year long – we're not playing the other team. We're playing ourselves. So we got to go out there and make sure that we're prepared and ready to go."

Far too often during the regular season, the Dodgers have managed to beat themselves, thanks to an unreliable bullpen. The ninth inning seemed to be going down that same dark alley.

"That was huge. We needed to," Dodgers catcher Will Smith said of changing the ending. "That would have really sucked for that one to get away."

It was about to, after Blake Treinen failed to retire any of the three batters he faced to start the ninth inning. A two-run double by Nick Castellanos made it a one-run game and put the tying run in scoring position.

When the infield gathered on the mound as Dodgers manager Dave Roberts brought in Alex Vesia to replace Treinen, a plan was hatched.

"The wheel play is not something that we traditionally do," Muncy said of a bunt defense that has both corner infielders crashing and the middle infielders covering first and third. "But as soon as we got in that situation, me, Mook and Tommy immediately started talking about, 'Hey, we got to try something different here.'

"And when Doc came out, made the pitching change, we talked to him about it, and he was all on board. I'm gonna credit Mook, because it was his idea. He was saying, 'We got to go wheel play. We got to go wheel play.' And so we talked about how we were going to do it, and we executed it to perfection."

It's something the Dodgers had practiced "not once" since spring training, Roberts said. But "for

Roki Sasaki helped the Dodgers avert disaster in the ninth inning by shutting down the Phillies' late rally. (AP Images)

Dodgers
11

LA
7
Rawlings

me, that was our only chance, really, to win that game in that moment."

The suggestion was coming from a player who had not played shortstop in the big leagues until last season.

"It's just a really smart baseball play," Muncy said. "And for him to immediately be coming right to me and talking about doing it, it shows his intuition in the game. He's second to none out there. It doesn't matter what position you put that guy at, he knows what's going on."

Bryson Stott dropped the bunt up the third-base line. Muncy fielded it quickly and without hesitation threw to third base where Betts had raced Castellanos to the base. He caught the throw and put the tag on Castellanos as he tumbled over him.

"It kept the tying run off third base, put it back on first base," Dodgers catcher Will Smith said. "That was probably the difference in the game today."

There was another difference - the Dodgers have a closer now. After Vesia gave up a single to Harrison Bader, a force out put runners at the corners for Trea Turner. Roki Sasaki came in and got Turner to ground out to second baseman Tommy Edman, with first baseman Freddie Freeman dropping to his knees to field Edman's one-hop throw behind the bag.

"The starting pitching is doing an amazing job results-wise," Sasaki said through his interpreter. "And all I'm trying to do is hold the lead or finish a game."

The starting pitching was amazing again - on both sides this time.

Blake Snell and Jesus Luzardo were brilliant through six scoreless innings, allowing just one hit each.

Teoscar Hernandez led off the seventh inning with a single then went to third on Freeman's double to right, chasing Luzardo and sparking a four-run inning.

The Dodgers' search for a solution to their unreliable bullpen led them to another dislocated starter. Emmet Sheehan followed Snell with a scoreless seventh but he ran into trouble in the eighth when he gave up a triple to Max Kepler and an RBI single to Turner.

Schwarber and Harper followed, and the Dodgers were carrying five lefties in the bullpen (Alex Vesia, Jack Dreyer, Tanner Scott, Anthony Banda and Clayton Kershaw). Roberts didn't call for any of them. Sheehan struck out Schwarber and got Harper on a harmless fly ball.

Those two dangerous hitters have gone 1 for 15 with eight strikeouts in the first two games of this NLDS.

"I think those guys are trying to do a little too much right now, instead of just being themselves and looking for base hits and the power will come," Phillies manager Rob Thomson said. ■

Blake Snell was terrific in the Game 2 win, pitching six scoreless innings with nine strikeouts. (AP Images)

National League Division Series Game 3
October 8, 2025 | Los Angeles, California
PHILLIES 8, DODGERS 2

'Pressure Is a Privilege'

Phillies' Offense Detonates to Beat Dodgers in Game 3, Extend Series

By Bill Plunkett

Tick, tick ... boom.

Kyle Schwarber exploded from his 0-for-22 slump with two home runs, the first a 455-foot 'Schwarbomb' that sparked the Philadelphia Phillies as they staved off elimination with an 8-2 victory over the Dodgers in Game 3 of their National League Division Series.

"I think we understand we're still up 2-1," Dodgers shortstop Mookie Betts said after being surrounded at his locker by cameras after the loss. "Obviously there's still a lot of pressure on us. But pressure is a privilege. Go out and play."

The loss was the Dodgers' first since Sept. 23 in Arizona, ending a nine-game winning streak that included their first four postseason games this year. They have another chance to close out the series at home.

"We just had a little quick meeting (before Game 3). Nothing crazy. But just focus on the game, win today," Phillies shortstop Trea Turner said after the win. "I think we all know we're kind of pressing as a group in the first two games and wanting to win so bad. And we know we're really good. We've just got to play like we always do. The message was just go 1-0 and worry about tomorrow tomorrow.

"I don't think anybody's feeling like it's our time to go home. We want to keep playing."

Schwarber and Bryce Harper had gone a combined 1 for 15 in the first two games of this series. They had four hits, two walks, three RBIs and three runs scored in Game 3.

"You make mistakes, you pitch behind, that's what's going to happen," Dodgers manager Dave Roberts said of Schwarber's rebirth.

"You've got to make pitches against those guys. They start getting some results and they start feeling good. We've got to make pitches and work ahead."

The National League's home run leader with 56 during the regular season – and the only possible threat to Shohei Ohtani winning a fourth league MVP award – Schwarber had started this series 0 for 7 with five strikeouts after ending the season hitless in his last 14 at-bats with eight more strikeouts.

He grounded out harmlessly in his first at-bat against Dodgers starter Yoshinobu Yamamoto. Leading off the fourth inning, though, Schwarber got a 2-and-0 fastball up over the plate and destroyed it. The ball left his bat at an Ohtani-like 117.2 mph and wasn't seen again until it had cleared the right field pavilion roof an estimated 455 feet from home plate.

"It's ridiculous how far that ball went," Turner said. "But I just think like the vibes, the energy, it's something to build off. Sometimes it's hard to create your own momentum. And you've got to build off things like that. No better way than the ball leaving the stadium."

Prior to that swing, the Phillies were hanging their hopes on powder-blue retro uniforms and escaping a hostile home environment where apparently the fans are too mean to them.

But Schwarber's blast gave them life. Bryce

Harper (1 for his first 7 in the series) followed with a single and Alec Bohm made it three consecutive hits when he singled to center field.

When Harper charged toward third base on Bohm's hit, Dodgers center fielder Andy Pages made a poor throw that bounced through third base, allowing Harper to score. The throw bounded into the dugout, allowing Bohm to go to third base and score on Brandon Marsh's sacrifice fly.

When Yamamoto gave up back-to-back singles in the fifth inning, his night was done. It was his shortest outing since failing to complete four innings against the New York Yankees on June 1.

"Getting into the game, I think I was calm," Yamamoto said through his interpreter. "But that fourth inning I allowed a solo run to Schwarber, and then after that I gave up more runs. If I could have minimized the damage in that inning, I think maybe the result might have been a little bit different."

The Phillies were met with skepticism and criticism on the Philadelphia airwaves after Manager Rob Thomson announced Aaron Nola, not Ranger Suarez as the Game 3 starter.

Unlike the Philly fan base, the Dodgers did not overreact to the decision, going with a lineup that looked more set for the lefty Suarez than the righty Nola.

It was the appropriate call – Nola lasted just two innings, essentially an extended opener for Suarez. The Dodgers had him on the ropes with a one-out triple by Mookie Betts in the first but they didn't score until Tommy Edman hit Suarez's first pitch of the night in the third inning over the wall in left field.

Thomson's combo-platter strategy might not have drawn the lineup reaction the Phillies were going for – but it got the results they needed. Nola and Suarez combined to allow just Edman's run in their combined seven innings.

"They pretty much did exactly what we wanted," Thomson said. "We wanted to use those guys to get as close to (closer Jhoan) Duran as we could to save some of the bullpen for tomorrow if we want.

"Nola was really good. The plan was to go one time through the lineup and Ranger is on Ohtani. We ended up with Edman leading off the third. He's 1-for-20 with nine strikeouts against Ranger, and he hit the first pitch out of the ballpark."

The Dodgers put two runners on with two outs in the fourth but Pages popped out. They got two on with one out in the sixth but Max Muncy bounced into a double play.

By the time Suarez handed the ball off to the bullpen in the eighth inning, the Phillies had started their fall raking, scoring five times on five hits – including home runs by JT Realmuto and Schwarber again (this time a wall-scraper) – off of Clayton Kershaw. Kershaw was pitching in the postseason for the first time since Game 1 of the 2023 NLDS and making his first postseason relief appearance since Game 5 of the 2019 NLDS. Neither of those went well either.

"He just didn't have a great slider tonight," Roberts said. "I think Clayton pitches off his slider. When the slider's not there – depthy, teethy ... then the fastball command, he was working behind, too. Just the command wasn't there tonight."

Kershaw gave up a hit and walked two (one intentionally) in the seventh, but Roberts sent him back out for the eighth in what was a two-run game, 3-1, before it blew up. Roberts revealed that Tanner Scott was not at the stadium for unspecified personal reasons, perhaps leading to the decision to send Kershaw back out for a second inning – and then leave him in as the inning unraveled.

"Tough couple innings there," Kershaw said. "I kind of got bailed out there in the seventh (by his defense). ... Just didn't make enough good pitches. I was battling command. It's hard when you're trying to throw strikes as opposed to getting people out. Just wasn't a fun inning." ■

National League Division Series Game 4
October 9, 2025 | Los Angeles, California
DODGERS 2, PHILLIES 1 (11)

'Pure Joy. A Little Bit of Laughter'

Unlikely Sequence in 11th Inning Sends Dodgers to NLCS

By Bill Plunkett

The hero was 1 for 24 in the series and had been dropped to ninth in the lineup for Game 4. The winning run was scored by the last player on the roster, playing in his first postseason game. The weakest link on the team has been shored up by a pitcher dominating at something he has never done before.

Two rookies and a second-year player – just like the Dodgers envisioned when they started writing $400 million worth of checks this year.

In danger of losing back-to-back games at home to send their National League Division Series back to Philadelphia to be decided, the Dodgers canceled their flight in the wackiest of ways, scoring the winning run in the 11th inning on a broken-bat comebacker that a panicked pitcher fired to the backstop.

The 2-1 victory in Game 4 over the Phillies sends the Dodgers on to the National League Championship Series for the fourth time in the past six years and the seventh time in the past 10 years under Manager Dave Roberts.

"It was just pure chaos," said second baseman Tommy Edman, who started the winning rally with a one-out single then watched his pinch-runner, Hyeseong Kim, score the winning run.

"Pure joy. A little bit of laughter because I wasn't sure what happened," said third baseman Max Muncy, running from second to third during the blooper reel that decided the game. "The way everyone was standing around I thought it was a foul ball at first. But then it just turned into pure joy. I looked over at Andy (Pages) and he's upset about a broken bat at first and then he realizes, 'Oh, I just won the game.'"

It was more like the Phillies lost the game.

There is no free runner on second to start extra innings in the postseason, so the Dodgers needed singles by Edman and Muncy to get things started in the 11th against against Phillies reliever Orion Kerkering. Kiké Hernandez drew a walk to load the bases with two outs and bring up Pages.

Roberts had pinch-hit for Pages in Game 3 and dropped him to ninth in the order for Game 4, a reaction to a slump that grew to 1 for 24 in the postseason. Kerkering got an 0-and-1 sinker in on Pages' hands, breaking his bat.

The ball skipped back to Kerkering who fumbled it off his foot, kicking it a few feet away. Panic set in. With catcher JT Realmuto pointing toward first base – "he would have been out," Dodgers first base coach Chris Woodward said of a play on Pages – Kerkering fired the ball home.

"I ran for my life. I just ran as hard as I could," Kim said through his interpreter.

Kerkering's throw was high and wide of the

Phillies pitcher Orion Kerkering finds himself in the middle of the Dodgers' celebration after Kerkering's throwing error allowed the Dodgers to score the winning run in the bottom of the 11th inning. (Los Angeles Daily News: Keith Birmingham)

Dodgers
51
Dodgers
17
BETTS
50

mark, not even close. Allowing Kim to score the series-clinching run.

"Once the pressure got to me, I just thought there's a faster throw to JT, a little quicker throw than trying to cross-body it to Bryce (Harper at first base)," Kerkering explained later. "So just a horse(bleep) throw.

"It's baseball. (Stuff) happens."

Stuff exploded out of the Dodgers' dugout with stunned looks on the faces of several players.

"It's one of those things that it's a PFP, a pitcher's fielding practice. He's done it a thousand times," Roberts said. "And right there he was so focused, I'm sure, on just getting the hitter and just sort of forgot the outs and the situation."

Pages saw Kerkering's bobble and kept running.

"Then I looked back and I saw that he threw home and I just thought, 'No, he threw the game away,'" Pages said in Spanish.

Even before its tragi-comic ending, Game 4 had enough October theater to require the extra-large tub of popcorn.

A scoreless duel between starters Tyler Glasnow and Cristopher Sanchez segued into late-inning tension. The Dodgers turned to their bullpen savior, Roki Sasaki, for three perfect innings in relief. With their backs to the wall, Phillies manager Rob Thomson tried to get an eight-out save from his closer, Jhoan Duran, then, a day after using two starters (Aaron Nola and Ranger Suarez) to stay alive, he used two more, bringing Jesus Luzardo (presumably their Game 5 starter) on in relief.

Glasnow held the Phillies scoreless for six innings but came out after just 83 pitches due to cramping. Emmet Sheehan followed and gave up the game's first run in the top of the seventh.

The Dodgers chased Sanchez from the game in the bottom of the seventh when a walk of Alex Call and a single by Kiké Hernandez put two runners on with one out. Thomson started pushing chips to the middle of the table when he went to his closer.

Duran got one out when Pages bounced to first. The runners advanced, giving Thomson another decision to make – should he use the open base to intentionally walk Ohtani? Despite Ohtani's 1-for-18 slump in this series, Thomson opted to walk him and load the bases for Betts.

Betts worked the count full, fouling off a 101.1 mph fastball to get there then taking a 101.4 mph fastball high for ball four to force in the tying run.

The game stayed tied as Sasaki faced nine batters and retired them all. Then Alex Vesia stranded a runner at second in the 11th.

"You're talking about one of the great all-time appearances out of the 'pen that I can remember," Roberts gushed of Sasaki. "Certainly given where he started this year, what he is as a starting pitcher, to go out there and not only go one inning, two innings and then three innings, and to do what he did gave us a huge boost.

"We're starting to see something really special in him, and that's why he was courted so hard in the offseason. But what he's done now on the biggest of stages, he's just scratching the surface."

All of that was just setting the stage for the crazy finish.

"I would much rather have seen a line drive in the gap or something," Dodgers catcher Will Smith said. "That's just pressure. It's pressure on them. It's pressure on us as well. He (Pages) did a good job of just moving the ball. You don't want to strike out there. Make them make a play. Keep pressure on them. And they didn't make the play." ■

Third baseman Kiké Hernandez catches a pop up off the bat of the Phillies' Bryce Harper in the eighth inning. (Los Angeles Daily News: Keith Birmingham)

8
Dodgers
44
17

76
SWEEP!
GUGGENHEIM
Spectrum
BANK OF AMERICA
TOYO TIRES
JINRO
Yakult
NATIONAL LEAGUE
CHAMPIONS
Dodgers
2025

NLCS

Los Angeles Daily News: Keith Birmingham

National League Championship Series Game 1
October 13, 2025 | Milwaukee, Wisconsin
DODGERS 2, BREWERS 1

A Clean Start

Blake Snell Stifles Brewers, Dodgers Hang On to Win NLCS Opener

By Bill Plunkett

Runs were harder to come by than low-fat cheese curds or a vegan bratwurst at American Family Field.

While Blake Snell was pitching a brilliant game on one side, the Milwaukee Brewers turned a head-spinning 404-foot double play on the other as the Dodgers and Brewers started their National League Championship Series with a 2-1 Dodgers victory in Game 1.

"He was amazing," Dodgers shortstop Mookie Betts said of Snell's dominant performance. "He put us on his back and he won it for us."

Snell faced the minimum 24 batters in eight scoreless innings, allowing one hit in the third inning and then picking the runner off. He was the first pitcher to face the minimum through eight innings of a postseason game since Don Larsen's perfect game during the 1956 World Series.

"He was electric," third baseman Max Muncy said. "He was lights-out. He had a really good idea of what he wanted to do out there and he executed to perfection."

The run prevention was elite on both sides. The only run in the first eight innings that couldn't be prevented was a solo home run by Freddie Freeman in the sixth.

The Dodgers didn't get their first hit of the game until the fourth inning. A leadoff walk of Teoscar Hernandez and back-to-back singles by Will Smith and Tommy Edman loaded the bases with one out for Muncy.

That's when things got confusing.

Muncy drove a fly ball over the wall in center field. Brewers center fielder Sal Frelick jumped and got a glove on it but the ball caromed off his glove and the top of the wall, bouncing back into the field of play – where Frelick caught it, thoroughly confusing the three Dodger baserunners.

"I didn't see it hit the wall," Smith said. "I just thought he kind of brought it back in and caught it. So I thought it was an out, maybe a sac fly. Obviously it hit the wall and that's not what happened."

At third base, Hernandez had tagged up when Muncy hit the fly ball. He left the base when Frelick made his leaping attempt but went back when the ball bounced off the wall and into Frelick's glove. That delay was enough for the relay throw from shortstop Joey Ortiz to beat Hernandez home, where catcher William Contreras had his foot on the base for a force out.

By rule, Hernandez could have headed home as soon as Frelick touched the ball – whether he caught it on the rebound or not.

"It happened fast," Dodgers manager Dave Roberts said. "I didn't know he didn't catch it, to be quite honest. We go over that rule. Teo knows the

Blake Snell faced the minimum 24 batters in eight scoreless innings, allowing one hit in the third inning as the Dodgers took a 1-0 series lead. (AP Images)

LA
THE GOLD GLOVE CO.
7

rule. I think right there he had just a little bit of a brain fart, appreciating that when it does hit the glove you can tag there. But then he tagged, did it correctly, then saw he didn't catch it, went back – that was the mistake."

Smith never tagged up at second on the initial play at the wall then headed back to second base when he thought Frelick had made the catch, waving at Edman (nearly at second base) to go back to first. Contreras trotted down to third base and touched the bag for a double play.

"With Sal running back, he gloves it first and it hits the wall. At that point it's no catch, right?" said crew chief James Hoye, who was at first base. "(Left field umpire) Chad (Fairchild), on that six-man system, it's his job to go out on that ball, from the left field line, to go out and get that ball.

"I see him (Fairchild) immediately saying no catch. They throw the ball in, and then all of a sudden you turn around and there's runners everywhere, right? At that point guys are going back, going forward. The coaches are spinning."

It took an on-field meeting of the entire umpiring crew and a replay review to sort things out.

"I obviously didn't see one signal. I just read it how I read it," Smith said.

"We went back and saw the left field ump was the one who called it. No one else called it. But I didn't think twice about it. I didn't think to look over there (for a call)."

The replay review confirmed Muncy's near-grand slam, potential sacrifice fly had turned into a 404-foot double play.

"I haven't seen any of the replays yet but you come out of that at-bat feeling good that you at least got one run on a sac fly," Muncy said. "I felt like I hit it good enough that it had a chance. Then you come away with nothing, a double play. It's definitely the worst fielder's choice, double play I've ever hit into in my life."

Snell needed none of the wackiness and very little help to put up his string of zeroes.

The Dodgers left-hander set the tone early. He threw 14 pitches in the first inning. The Brewers swung and missed at six of them.

In all, the Brewers swung 49 times at Snell's pitches, missing nearly half (22) of the time on their way to 10 strikeouts. Snell's changeup was particularly effective, getting 14 of those swing-and-misses.

"He was great. His sequencing in terms of throwing his changeup is effective," Brewers manager Pat Murphy said, giving credit to Smith as well for that sequencing. "His changeup and slider were incredible. The kid is incredible. I've seen him pitch like that before.

"I think it's the most dominant performance against us. I've been here 10 years. ... The kid was amazing."

In three starts this postseason, Snell has allowed just two runs (in the seventh inning of Wild Card Series Game 1 against the Cincinnati Reds) on six hits over 21 innings. The Reds, Philadelphia Phillies and Brewers have hit .090 (6 for 67) while striking out 28 times.

"I pitch off of what they're telling me," Snell said of his changeup-heavy domination of the Brewers. "I just felt like they were really aggressive to a certain pitch (his fastball) and it seemed to be that way. So I threw differently."

Snell was so unpressured that he completed eight innings on 103 pitches, allowing Roberts to make the pitching change of his dreams, going from Snell to Roki Sasaki for the ninth inning, though he considered sending Snell back out.

"I thought it was 50/50," Roberts said. "Roki has been throwing the baseball really well. We have a two-run lead. I felt good with Roki there."

Betts had given the Dodgers that two-run lead by drawing a walk after the Brewers had intentionally walked Shohei Ohtani in the top of the ninth, loading the bases with one out.

Freddie Freeman doubles in the eighth inning of Game 1, his second extra-base hit of the night after hitting a solo home run in the sixth. (AP Images)

"It wasn't as hard a decision as you think, because when a bag's open and you can turn it into a double-play situation, you've got a right-hander on the mound (reliever Abner Uribe), you kind of have to go for that," Murphy said. "Shohei is at least dangerous enough, struggling or not, he's dangerous enough to hit a fly ball. And you can't give up the run there. With the way we were swinging against Snell, we couldn't give up a run."

After three perfect innings in the closeout game against the Phillies, Sasaki's velocity was down and his command was off. He walked Isaac Collins with one out then gave up a ground-rule double to Jake Bauers, the bounce over the wall saving a run. The Brewers cashed that one in on a sacrifice fly by Jackson Chourio. When Sasaki walked Christian Yelich, Roberts went looking for another bullpen hero.

"He was just a little off," Roberts said. "I thought his stuff was still good, but just missing. I don't know if there was carry-over from the three innings."

Blake Treinen came on and walked William Contreras to load the bases before striking out Brice Turang to end the game on a pitch well above the strike zone.

"Out of hand, I was a little bit frustrated," Treinen said of the last pitch of the game. "But when he swung, I was a little more happy." ■

National League Championship Series Game 2

October 14, 2025 | Milwaukee, Wisconsin

DODGERS 5, BREWERS 1

Old-School Dominance

Yoshinobu Yamamoto Throws First MLB Postseason Complete Game in Eight Years

By Bill Plunkett

Like D.I.Y. shoppers at Menards, the Dodgers got everything they came for in Milwaukee.

Relying on their starting pitching to do the heavy lifting, the Dodgers came away with a 5-1 victory over the Milwaukee Brewers in Game 2 of the National League Championship Series and headed back to L.A. having stolen home-field advantage.

The Brewers need to take two out of three at Dodger Stadium in order to send the series back to Milwaukee. Tyler Glasnow is scheduled to start Game 3 for the Dodgers.

He will have two tough acts to follow.

Blake Snell's historically dominant performance in Game 1 was followed by the first postseason complete game from a Dodgers pitcher since Jose Lima pitched a five-hit shutout in the 2004 NL Division Series against the St. Louis Cardinals. Yoshinobu Yamamoto, who gave up a home run on the first pitch he threw in Game 2, allowed just two singles over his next 110. It was the first postseason complete game since Justin Verlander threw one for the Houston Astros against the New York Yankees in 2017 and the first in the NLCS since Josh Beckett for the then-Florida Marlins in 2003.

"The last two nights have been impressive by those two. It's been incredible," Dodgers catcher Will Smith said. "That's probably the two best back-to-back games pitched ever, that I've seen."

Brewers manager Pat Murphy wasn't about to argue.

"Both those pitchers were as dominant as two pitchers have been," Murphy said. "We chased way more than we've chased all year. We've been the best in baseball at not chasing. These pitchers brought out the worst in us.

"The ball-strike (discipline) has been really at the core of our offensive success, and sometimes great pitching brings out the worst in you. ... Both guys were dominant for 17 innings. So hats off to those two guys. They deserve all the credit. They really do. They deserve all the credit."

A plan has come together.

The Dodgers' desire to ride their starting pitching in October and minimize the exposure of their Achilles' heel (the bullpen) is being fulfilled. Eight games into their postseason (seven wins), their starting pitchers – Shohei Ohtani, Snell, Yamamoto and Glasnow – have gobbled up 52⅔ innings while allowing 11 runs (nine earned) on 24 hits and striking out 63.

"It's been incredible," third baseman Max Muncy said. "Blake was historic last night and then for Yama to come out tonight – he gives up a leadoff homer. For him, he's probably sitting there thinking, 'Crap, not again' but then he goes out and completes the game.

"It's just really awesome to see these guys go out there. You're right – we said before the postseason we were going to ride our starting pitching and

Yoshinobu Yamamoto allowed just three hits and one run in MLB's first postseason complete game since 2017. (AP Images)

LA

that's what we've been doing. I definitely think that's what we're going to continue to do. They're our strength. I think this is what the front office was imagining when they went out and signed these guys. It's obviously a long season. You're going to deal with injuries and not everyone's always going to be healthy. Realistically, the last month and a half of the season, this is what we were seeing."

Jackson Chourio did ambush a first-pitch fastball from Yamamoto to lead off the bottom of the first inning with an opposite-field home run and raise the specter of Yamamoto's July start at American Family Field. He didn't make it out of the first inning that day.

He accomplished that in Game 3 with three consecutive ground outs after Chourio's home run, then worked around an error by Muncy in the second inning and two-out singles in the third and fourth innings. He walked his only batter of the night with one out in the fifth inning after an odd mound visit from Smith and pitching coach Mark Prior with Dodgers manager Dave Roberts standing near the foul line, anticipating a physical issue.

Yamamoto sent them away and retired the final 14 Brewers in order after walking Joey Ortiz.

"That was the first hitter and I felt regrettable, that home run," Yamamoto said through his interpreter. "But I reset my mind and then I just focused on executing my pitches."

Yamamoto relied on his splitter, throwing it more than any other pitch (33 of his 111 pitches) and getting half of his 14 swings-and-misses with it.

"It was really good tonight," Smith said. "It was kind of inning-to-inning. Some innings it wasn't biting as much. We kind of did some other things. Some innings it was. We just kind of leaned on it. He was just executing. He kind of had everything going. His curveball was good. The fastball, cutter were pretty good. He was just mixing and throwing strikes and putting guys away."

After being overwhelmed by Snell's changeup, in particular, in Game 1, the Brewers weren't up to the challenge of Yamamoto's deep pitch mix.

"This guy's split looks like a heater," Murphy said. "It comes out of the same tunnel. It looks exactly the same. He's got an impeccable delivery. He doesn't miss a lot. And the ball shows up as a heater – bang, goes down. And his heater shows up as a heater and then rises. So it's pretty impressive.

"It's been put in our face now for two days, two great performances. But that doesn't mean the series is over."

The Dodgers took a 2-1 lead in the second inning then eventually added to it.

At the center of Game 1's most-dissected double play when he tagged up twice, Teoscar Hernandez tagged Freddy Peralta for a solo home run in the second inning. Kiké Hernandez singled with two outs and scored from first when Andy Pages doubled down the right field line. That followed a 1-for-27 start to the postseason for Pages.

The instigator of Game 1's most talked about play when Brewers center fielder Sal Frelick brought his fly ball back into play, Muncy cleared both the center field fence and Frelick's glove for a solo home run in the sixth inning.

The home run was Muncy's 14th in postseason play, breaking a tie with Justin Turner and Corey Seager for the most in franchise history.

"It means a lot to me," said Muncy, who has made no secret of his desire to finish his career with the Dodgers. "The Dodgers are a franchise that has been around for a very, very long time. A lot of very successful players have played in this organization. And to be able to break that record is kind of huge for me.

"But the biggest thing I would say is it speaks to the fact that I've had a chance to play in so many postseason games. And that's the biggest thing about being a Dodger, you know you'll have a chance in October to play meaningful baseball games."

An inning later, Kiké Hernandez doubled and scored when another slumping teammate got a hit – Ohtani slapped a single through the drawn-in Brewers infield to bring Hernandez home. Ohtani was 1 for 23 with 11 strikeouts before that hit. ■

Shohei Ohtani's seventh-inning RBI single put the Dodgers up 4-1. (AP Images)

STRAUSS

National League Championship Series Game 3
October 16, 2025 | Los Angeles, California
DODGERS 3, BREWERS 1

Confidence Game

Dodgers' Bullpen Delivers Against Brewers for 3-0 Lead

By Bill Plunkett

In much of the country, the leaves are turning. In California, it might be the Dodgers' bullpen that has changed colors – from flashing red to cautionary yellow.

With Tyler Glasnow pulled in the sixth inning, the Dodgers were left counting outs on trembling hands. They got 10 of them from four relievers who made a two-run lead stand up for a 3-1 victory over the Milwaukee Brewers in Game 3 of the National League Championship Series.

"The starting pitchers have been amazing," Dodgers reliever Alex Vesia said. "Last year, it was the bullpen 'dawgs' and this year I think the starters have definitely been the bread and butter. It's awesome, man. Watching them do their thing – I'm grinning and smiling ear to ear.

"To go eight innings, next guy goes nine (Blake Snell and Yoshinobu Yamamoto in Games 1 and 2) – I mean, yeah, it was good to get in there. I think that was a huge confidence boost for all of us. We'll just keep clicking them off one at a time, leaning on each other. I think that's what this group does so special. Today was a great win."

It was the Dodgers' eighth win in nine postseason games, 13th in their past 14th overall and 23rd in their past 29 games. They will go for a sweep of the Brewers with Shohei Ohtani on the mound for Game 4.

"We're up," said shortstop Mookie Betts, who followed a leadoff triple by Shohei Ohtani with an RBI double to produce the Dodgers' first run. "But you know, like Kobe (Bryant) said, the job's not done, so we've got to keep going and just keep applying pressure."

The Brewers were supposed to apply pressure on the Dodgers with an offense that put the ball in play consistently and ran the bases aggressively. They have managed three runs on nine hits while striking out 30 times in the first three games of this series.

"That team is pretty good. So are we," Brewers manager Pat Murphy said. "We haven't shown our best foot. Like I said, if you would have told me the Dodgers would score 10 runs in three games, what would be the (series) score? If you said 2-1 us, or 1-2 them – you wouldn't say 0-3.

"But we haven't got the clutch hit. We've been a little bit foreign to how we've played in terms of contact."

The Dodgers haven't let them get the clutch hit. They didn't even have their first at-bat with a runner in scoring position against a Dodgers starter until the first inning of Game 3. With one out in the second, Caleb Durbin sent a drive into left field that Kiké Hernandez turned into a triple when his diving attempt came up short. Durbin scored when Jake Bauers hit a single through the middle of a drawn-in infield.

Bauers stole second and went to third on an errant pickoff attempt by Glasnow. But third baseman Max Muncy saved a run when he handled Joey Ortiz's ground ball to his left, popping up and throwing Bauers out at home.

"That was huge," said Glasnow, who retired 12 of 13 after Ortiz's ground ball. "I think that was the play of the game, for sure. Just having a one-run ball game, if it had turned into two, it's a different story."

Game 3's mid-afternoon start suited TV but made things even more difficult for hitters as shadows passed in front of the plate, eventually to the outfield. Eleven of 19 batters struck out against Glasnow and hard-throwing Milwaukee rookie Jacob Misiorowski in the third, fourth and fifth innings with just one baserunner (on a walk), leaving the game locked in a 1-1 tie until the Dodgers put something together in the sixth.

"That was not fun," Dodgers catcher Will Smith said. "Even catching, I know what's coming but it's still hard to catch. The at-bats were even harder. That's kind of one of those games within the games – who can handle it better? We got to Misiorowski late there."

Smith started it with a one-out single in the sixth. Freddie Freeman worked a walk – he and Misiorowski each working the pitch clock. Tommy Edman followed with a single through the middle to drive in the go-ahead run.

"Just watching that inning, it felt like the shadows had finally gone deep enough that guys were seeing the ball a bit better," Muncy said. "He's obviously got unbelievable stuff. I don't want to take anything away from that. He was throwing really well today. He was locating, he was mixing his pitches well. And on top of that, you add in the visuals. It was very tough. But that inning, it just felt like guys were seeing the ball a little bit better. And yeah, Tommy coming through right there, that was huge."

That was it for Misiorowski. Murphy called on one of his high-leverage relievers to put out the fire. Freeman had pushed the envelope and went from first base to third successfully on Edman's single. That proved critical when Abner Uribe made a wild pickoff attempt on Edman at first, allowing Freeman to trot home with a second run.

Vesia had replaced Glasnow after a two-out walk in the top of the sixth pushed the starter's pitch count to 99. Vesia got Sal Frelick to end that inning but gave up a leadoff double to Caleb Durbin to start the seventh. He got Bauers to fly out. Blake Treinen got the next two outs.

After Anthony Banda pitched a 1-2-3 eighth, Roki Sasaki came on for the ninth. His first pitch was a reassuring 99.7 mph after his velocity had slipped in Game 1. He attributed the drop in velocity to getting slightly out of his mechanics not fatigue from the three-inning outing to close out the NL Division Series.

"As a starter, I understand that there's always ups and downs," Sasaki said through his interpreter. "So, I kind of take that same approach with pitching as a reliever. And I think what I try to do is just to make sure that everything, all my mechanics are in place so that I can command the ball better. And I feel like that's what I'm really focused on right now."

Betts made a Gold Glove finalist-worthy play for the first out – ranging into the hole to make a backhand play then a jump throw to first. A pop out and a strikeout settled things with none of the drama the bullpen provided far too often during the regular season.

"We've been telling them all year that we believe in them," Muncy said of the bullpen's performance. "Hopefully they're getting a little confidence and they start believing in themselves. But yeah, we trust them. Every time we see them come running through the gate, everyone on the infield trusts that they're coming in to do their job, and that's never been an issue. They're pitching how we've expected." ■

Smart Spenders

Dodgers' Payroll Dwarfs Most of Their Peers, but They Get Their Money's Worth

By Mirjam Swanson | October 16, 2025

Shoutout to all the pocket-watching haters. All the poor schmucks crying foul ball; that it's just not fair!

Baseball needs a salary cap! Someone needs to rein in the Dodgers! With their Guggenheim Baseball Management consortium, they're just too rich! As if *that* ain't rich coming from anyone supporting the ball club that barged into the postseason with the best record in baseball.

It's not that complaints are falling on deaf ears here in L.A., it's that the chorus of complaints are music to Dodger fans' ears. Cry harder, in fact; L.A. is loving this song. Loving having an ownership group that does everything it can – and most everything right – to help the Dodgers win.

Because, yes, the Dodgers have awoken from their regular-season hibernation and now find themselves right where they planned to be: One victory from a second consecutive trip to the World Series, hungry.

After sweeping the Cincinnati Reds in their Wild Card Series and making quick work of the Philadelphia Phillies in the National League Division Series, Goliath beat David again Thursday in the NLCS. The Dodgers' 3-1 victory in Game 3 gave them a commanding 3-0 lead in the best-of-seven NL Championship Series.

Those "Above Average Joe's" playing for Milwaukee – as Manager Pat Murphy recently called his fellas – now are on the verge of an NLCS appearance that lasts only about as long as it takes to get a cup of joe.

It isn't the NLCS slugfest so many wanted. It's not setting to be a seven-game showcase between the star-studded favorites and the plucky underdogs on the other side. It's looking, instead, like we might just get a sweep.

How dare the Dodgers bully the 97-win Brewers like this? How dare baseball's reigning champions step up to the plate and play like champions against the club that beat them all six times they met in the regular season?

How dare the Dodgers figure it out when it matters most.

How dare they operate so smartly. Out-competence the competition. Get their money's worth – make sure their major-league-leading $350 million payroll pays off.

Does their payroll significantly exceed the small-market Brewers' $122 million? Quite. Does it dwarf completely what the Chicago White Sox ($78.8 million) and Oakland A's ($78.3 million) and Miami Marlins ($67.9 million) are paying their players? Totally.

But ask yourself, is it the Dodgers who are Bad For Baseball or the cheapskate bottom-dwellers unwilling to invest what it takes to compete?

Also, pop quiz: Don't the New York Mets have essentially the same payroll as the Dodgers? Yes, they do – $342 million. Do they feel like virtual shoo-ins for the World Series? No, they don't. They didn't even make the playoffs this year, despite signing Juan Soto to a $765 million deal.

Elsewhere in the NL, this season the Arizona Diamondbacks added ace right-hander Corbin Burnes on a $210 million deal and the San Francisco Giants spent $182 million for shortstop Willy Adames, and neither team made the postseason.

Shoot, there's an NBA team around here with no titles despite having allegedly paid more than permitted by a salary cap – further proof, possibly, that there are no guarantees, that you have to have good fortune on your side too, that maybe you have to go

Two-time Cy Young Award winner Blake Snell signed a five-year deal with the Dodgers following the 2024 season. (Los Angeles Daily News: Keith Birmingham)

about things the right way.

So, yes, this past offseason, the Dodgers picked up two-time Cy Young Award winner Blake Snell on a five-year deal, paying him an annual salary of about $36.4 million – "heck," Murphy said the other day, "Snell makes more money than our entire pitching staff."

But Snell – who faced the minimum amount of Milwaukee hitters possible in Game 1 before being pulled after the eighth inning and who looks lined up to start Game 5, if we get that far – could've made a similar amount had he opted into the final year of his deal with the Giants.

Why'd he choose to leave and come to L.A.? "This is where you want to play," he said.

Same reason Japanese sensation Roki Sasaki – who has emerged as the Dodgers' surprise solution at closer – brought his talents here.

The Dodgers scored highest on the "homework assignment" he gave all his MLB suitors, none of whom could outlandishly outspend the others because Sasaki is considered an international amateur by MLB's rules and could only sign a minor-league contract with a limited signing bonus.

"Right in our wheelhouse," Dodgers president of baseball operations Andrew Friedman said of the assignment. "Our ability to showcase our performance-science group, our training staff, our performance staff, our pitching coaches, how connected those groups are, we felt like really highlighted a strength of ours."

Athletes will always want to go where they can win, where they trust they'll be put in the best position to win. Build a winner, and winners will come.

Sorry, not sorry. ■

National League Championship Series Game 4
October 17, 2025 | Los Angeles, California
DODGERS 5, BREWERS 1

'The Shohei Ohtani Game'

Dodgers' Superstar Hits Three Home Runs and Pitches Six Scoreless Innings to Seal NLCS Sweep

By Bill Plunkett

You don't tug on Superman's cape.

The buzzing of doubt was thick around Shohei Ohtani after a 1-for-18 National League Division Series and a 2-for-11 start to the NL Championship Series, enough to make Ohtani sound a little annoyed by the tone of the questions at a press conference on Wednesday.

He swatted those doubts away Friday as only he can.

Making his first pitching start since Game 1 of the NL Division Series, Ohtani struck out the side in the top of the first inning then led off the bottom of the first by slamming a 446-foot home run. He didn't give up a hit until the fourth inning, hit a second home run even farther, added a third home run and struck out 10 while taking a shutout into the seventh inning as the Dodgers beat the Milwaukee Brewers, 5-1, on Thursday night, completing a sweep of the NLCS.

If Ohtani's 6-for-6, three-home run game to create the 50/50 club last year might have been the greatest offensive game ever, Game 4's two-way domination has to be considered for status as the greatest postseason performance.

"Sometimes you've got to check yourself and touch him to make sure he's not just made of steel," said first baseman Freddie Freeman, last season's World Series MVP. "Absolutely incredible. Biggest stage, and he goes out and does something like that. It'll probably be remembered as the Shohei Ohtani game."

Pitching coach Mark Prior said it was the kind of performance you might see "probably like (in) the Little League World Series" not at the major-league level.

"That stuff ends usually in high school," Prior said. "It's unbelievable."

Dodgers president of baseball operations Andrew Friedman didn't hesitate, calling it "the greatest postseason performance ever."

"I think there's no question about it," Friedman said. "Through four innings I texted our Slack thread and said, 'This is the greatest four innings ever played in postseason history by a major-league player. The greatest four innings ever.' Then he hits another home run. 'The greatest six innings ever. Seven innings.' There's no question it was the greatest postseason performance ever.

"He woke up this morning with people questioning him and 12 hours later he's standing on the podium as the NLCS MVP. It speaks volumes about the game he had and the talent he has."

There were none of those doubts in the Dodgers' dugout.

"You guys asked me yesterday and I said I was expecting nothing short of incredible today. And he proved me wrong. He went beyond incredible," third baseman Max Muncy said. "I don't know what I saw

Shohei Ohtani pumps his fist after striking out Milwaukee's Jake Bauers to end the fourth inning of Game 4. Ohtani had 10 strikeouts in six scoreless innings. (Los Angeles Daily News: Keith Birmingham)

LA
Dodgers
17

today. That was beyond incredible. The first home run, I didn't think he could top that then he hits one literally out of the stadium. ... It went over the roof, which means it came really close to hitting the scoreboard. I've played a lot of games here. I've never seen a ball go that far. I know Statcast said 460 feet, but Statcast is wrong. That ball was at least 500 feet."

"There's only one person who can do that in the world, and in the history of this game, and it's him," Kiké Hernandez said.

With that, the Dodgers are going to the World Series for the fifth time in the past nine years, the Brewers having offered minimal resistance in the NLCS. The Dodgers are the first defending champions to make it back to the World Series since the Philadelphia Phillies won it all in 2008 then lost to the New York Yankees in the 2009 World Series.

The Dodgers will try to become the first team to win consecutive World Series titles since the Yankees in 1998-2000.

"This is a one-team, one-dream operation," Dodgers manager Dave Roberts said on the podium, raising the NL championship trophy. "Before this season they were saying the Dodgers are ruining baseball. Let's get four more wins and really ruin baseball."

They arrive at a World Series appearance that seemed to be preordained by their $400 million payroll and accumulation of talent with as much momentum as ever. They have won nine of 10 postseason games and 24 of their past 30 overall.

"Every year in spring training, every team probably has a similar speech," Muncy said. "'We're here to work. Our goal is to win the World Series.' The reality of it is, there's only a couple of teams where that's the truth. With us, that's the truth every single year. Our goal is to win the World Series. That's what we expect. Anything less than that is a failure.

"For us, showing up to spring this year it was, 'Hey, we need to repeat.' It wasn't like we wanted to repeat. It was like, 'Hey, we need to repeat.'"

Asked why it was "need to repeat" and not just want to repeat, Muncy said, "Because that's just how good we are."

The six-day layoff before Game 1 of the World Series figures to provide more of a challenge to that momentum than the Brewers did despite their status as MLB's winningest team during the regular season. Dodgers pitching held the Brewers to four runs on 14 hits in the four-game sweep.

Ohtani walked Brice Turang to start the game, luring the Brewers into believing he might be human. He struck out the next three to sow doubt and didn't give up a hit until Jackson Chourio led off the fourth inning with a ground-rule double.

Ohtani took care of that threat with a ground out and two more strikeouts. He walked the first batter in the seventh inning and gave up a single, ending his night on the mound at 100 pitches with no runs, only two hits and three walks allowed. He left the mound to a stadium-shaking ovation.

"I really focused on, first of all, first and foremost, as a starting pitcher to make sure I'm an effective starting pitcher," Ohtani said through his interpreter. "On the hitting side, looking at the whole entire team, we will see that at times the right-handed hitters picked us up. And on the flip side, sometimes the left-handed hitters picked us up. So in a sense we're just trying to find the right balance."

His first home run was part of a three-run first inning for the Dodgers. Mookie Betts, Will Smith and Tommy Edman had singles to produce one run and another scored on Teoscar Hernandez's slow ground out to first.

Lightning struck again with two outs in the fourth when Brewers reliever Chad Patrick fell behind, 3-and-1, to Ohtani. He threw a cutter that was actually off the plate inside. It was nearly hit off the planet.

Ohtani crushed it, sending it over the pavilion roof

Shohei Ohtani watches his leadoff home run in the bottom of the first inning of Game 4. At the plate, Ohtani hit three home runs in the Dodgers' pennant-clinching win. (Los Angeles Daily News: Keith Birmingham)

anDepot
2025
LCS
loanDepot
Dodgers

in right field, an estimated 469 feet (which didn't seem to do it justice). The ball left his bat at 116.9 mph, topping the 116.5 mph of his first home run and leaving teammates in the dugout throwing their arms to the sky in amazement. The ball bounced off the pavilion roof and into a bush near some tables where startled fans were eating.

"That's the farthest ball I've ever seen hit," Muncy said. "I've seen a lot of games here at Dodger Stadium and that's not even close. It's the farthest ball I've ever seen hit.

"It's kind of funny. There wasn't one person in the dugout that didn't think he was going to hit a home run. He hits the second one and we're all talking, 'Is this the single greatest game anyone has ever played?' Everyone at the same time just said, 'You know he's going to hit another one.'"

He did.

In the seventh inning, Ohtani made it a threesome, sending a 99-mph fastball from Trevor Megill out to left center. The three home runs covered 1,342 feet – a little over a quarter-mile. A pitcher had hit three home runs in a game (any game, regular or postseason) just once before – Jim Tobin of the Boston Braves in May 1932.

"There was a lot of talk that he was scuffling at the plate, he doesn't swing the bat well when he's pitching. And all those things I think were fuel to his fire," Roberts said. "So today when he took the mound, you can see the focus, the intent. And after that shutdown first inning, just the at-bat right there, you could see that he was smelling a really good night tonight."

Ohtani, a three-time league MVP who is favored to win a fourth next month, is the 12th player to hit three homers in a postseason game and the first since Chris Taylor did it for the Dodgers in October 2021.

"We're like the (Chicago) Bulls and he's Michael Jordan," Betts said. ■

Teammates high-five Shohei Ohtani in the Dodgers' dugout after Ohtani's leadoff home run in the bottom of the first inning. In the top half of that frame, Ohtani struck out three Brewers batters. (Los Angeles Daily News: Keith Birmingham)

ULTRA
Security Benefit
UCLA Health
DAISO
Dodgers
17
LOS ANGELES

The Best Ever?

Shohei Ohtani Authors an Unforgettable Night at Chavez Ravine

By Mirjam Swanson | October 17, 2025

There aren't enough superlatives left to describe this man, this myth, this legend. And we can't print curse words in the newspaper, so ...

So here's what I've got: Shohei. Ohtani.

If you read that name, you know what I'm sayin': It simply doesn't get any greater than.

The GOAT; the GOAT.

The greatest player of all time having the greatest game of all time – in no small part because of the great time he picked to have it: Game 4 of the National League Championship Series, World Series berth there for the taking.

Three home runs.

Ten strikeouts.

Six scoreless innings.

By one guy! By the same guy!

Stuff of legends, stuff of gods.

Stuff of envy, stuff of awe.

Said first baseman Freddie Freeman: "I'm still speechless."

Echoed fellow ace pitcher Blake Snell: "That was crazy."

Manager Dave Roberts: "He created a lot of memories for a lot of people."

And anyone got any questions anymore about whether he can hit if he pitches in a postseason game? Anyone? Anybody? No? So that's settled. Ohtani settled it.

The 10-year, $700 million man exploded out of his postseason slump, picked up the Dodgers and launched them back into the World Series with an unprecedented pinch-me performance in a 5-1 victory to sweep the Milwaukee Brewers on an unforgettable night at Chavez Ravine.

Ohtani hadn't been his best self coming into play; between the four-game series victory over the Philadelphia Phillies in the NL Division Series and the first three games of the NLCS, Ohtani was 3 for 29 (.103) without a homer, only a pair of RBIs, 14 strikeouts and five walks – three of which were intentional.

But a few hours before Ohtani's first pitch on Friday, Roberts wasn't worried.

"This is his opportunity to make his mark on this series," Roberts predicted. "We're going to see his best effort. I feel good that he's pitching for us. And there's going to be some serious focus and compete tonight."

No, but seriously. The NLCS MVP and soon-to-be four-time league MVP, baseball's undisputed unicorn gouged the overmatched Brewers hitters with his nasty array of pitches.

The 31-year-old right-handed pitcher used his cutter, his sweeper, his slider and his heat – a four-seam fastball that touched 100 mph early and remained in the high-90s. He threw 100 pitches and allowed just two hits, the fourth Dodgers pitcher to completely confound Milwaukee in the series sweep.

But then there was Ohtani's Superman quick changes from hurler to slugger, his transformation into the Dodgers' leadoff hitter who this season hit a personal- and franchise-record 55 home runs.

In the first inning, Ohtani the hitter worked the count full against Milwaukee starter Jose Quintana and then homered to right field – the first home run by a Dodgers pitcher in the postseason.

He was feeling good.

In his next at-bat in the fourth inning, he crushed his second – the longest hit in the Statcast era, 469 feet, beyond the right-field pavilion roof – something only Willie Stargell and Kyle Schwarber had done.

Previously, only one pitcher in postseason

Shohei Ohtani made a case for the greatest baseball game of all time in Game 4 of the NLCS, striking out 10 in six scoreless innings on the mound while hitting three home runs at the plate. (Los Angeles Daily News: Keith Birmingham)

history had 10 or more strikeouts and a homer in a game: Bob Gibson, twice.

Good company, for sure. Except that Ohtani – *the* greatest – doesn't need any.

He hit his third bomb – a 427-foot shot to center field – in the seventh inning, pushing the Dodgers' lead to 5-0 and sending the stadium into delirium.

There was a guy – a right-hander named Jim Tobin – who pitched for the Boston Braves and hit three home runs in a big league game back on May 13, 1942, when Major League Baseball had lost many of its stars like Joe DiMaggio and Ted Williams to military service.

Otherwise, nobody else and never before.

"He's just too talented, and it's not like the moment's ever too big for him," Roberts said afterward. "So with that combination, you just know that it's going to happen at some point."

Thing is, "it" can mean just about anything when it comes to Ohtani. You don't even have to be able to dream it and he still might pull *it* off.

Ohtani is only the 12th hitter to go deep three times in a postseason game, though the players on that list – Babe Ruth, twice, and Dodgers Chris Taylor and Kiké Hernandez, included – weren't also pitching those games.

There had previously been only 24 home runs hit by pitchers in a playoff game.

So what about Ohtani vs. Ohtani, historically? Mirror, mirror, that might be the only fair comp for the man who Roberts correctly calls "the greatest player on the planet."

On June 27, 2023, Ohtani started for the Angels, got the win – giving up one run in 6⅓ innings – over the Chicago White Sox and hit two home runs.

A pretty, pretty, pretty good game.

And then there was July 27, 2023, when the Angels played two. In the first game of the doubleheader, Ohtani pitched a one-hitter in nine innings in a 6-0 victory over Detroit. Then in Game 2, he came right back and hit two home runs in the Halos' 11-4 victory.

A pretty, pretty, pretty good day.

But not as good as Friday. Nowhere as great as Friday.

Game 4 was something to toast to, said Ohtani himself, telling his ecstatic "M-V-P!"-chanting fans who hung around to watch him get his NLCS MVP hardware: "I hope everybody in L.A. and Japan and all over the world can enjoy a really good sake."

Cheers to that. Cheers to Shohei Ohtani. ■